GRENDEL

THE Devil Inside

Creator • Writer • Cover Artist

MATT WAGNER

Artist

BERNIE MIREAULT

DIANA SCHUTZ

TIM ERVIN-GORE • JEREMY BARLOW

AMY ARENDTS • CARY GRAZZINI

JASON HVAM • RICH POWERS

MIKE RICHARDSON

GRENDEL™: THE DEVIL INSIDE

This book collects issues one through three of the Dark Horse comic book series *Grendel: The Devil Inside*.

Published by
Dark Horse Books
A division of Dark Horse Comics, Inc.
10956 SE Main Street
Milwaukie, Oregon 97222

www.darkhorse.com

First edition: February 2004
ISBN: 1-56971-604-8

1 3 5 7 9 10 8 6 4 2

PRINTED IN CHINA

GRENDEL

THE Devil Inside

Brian Li Sung watched his lover, Christine Spar, die at the
bloody hands of Argent the Wolf, a victim of the notorious Grendel
legacy. Shortly thereafter, he received the original Grendel
logs written by Hunter Rose, along with Christine's own journals,
in the mail. Having chosen to stay on in New York,
rather than return to his native San Francisco, Brian finds himself
at the mercy of the pitiless city — and perhaps at the mercy
of something more sinister …

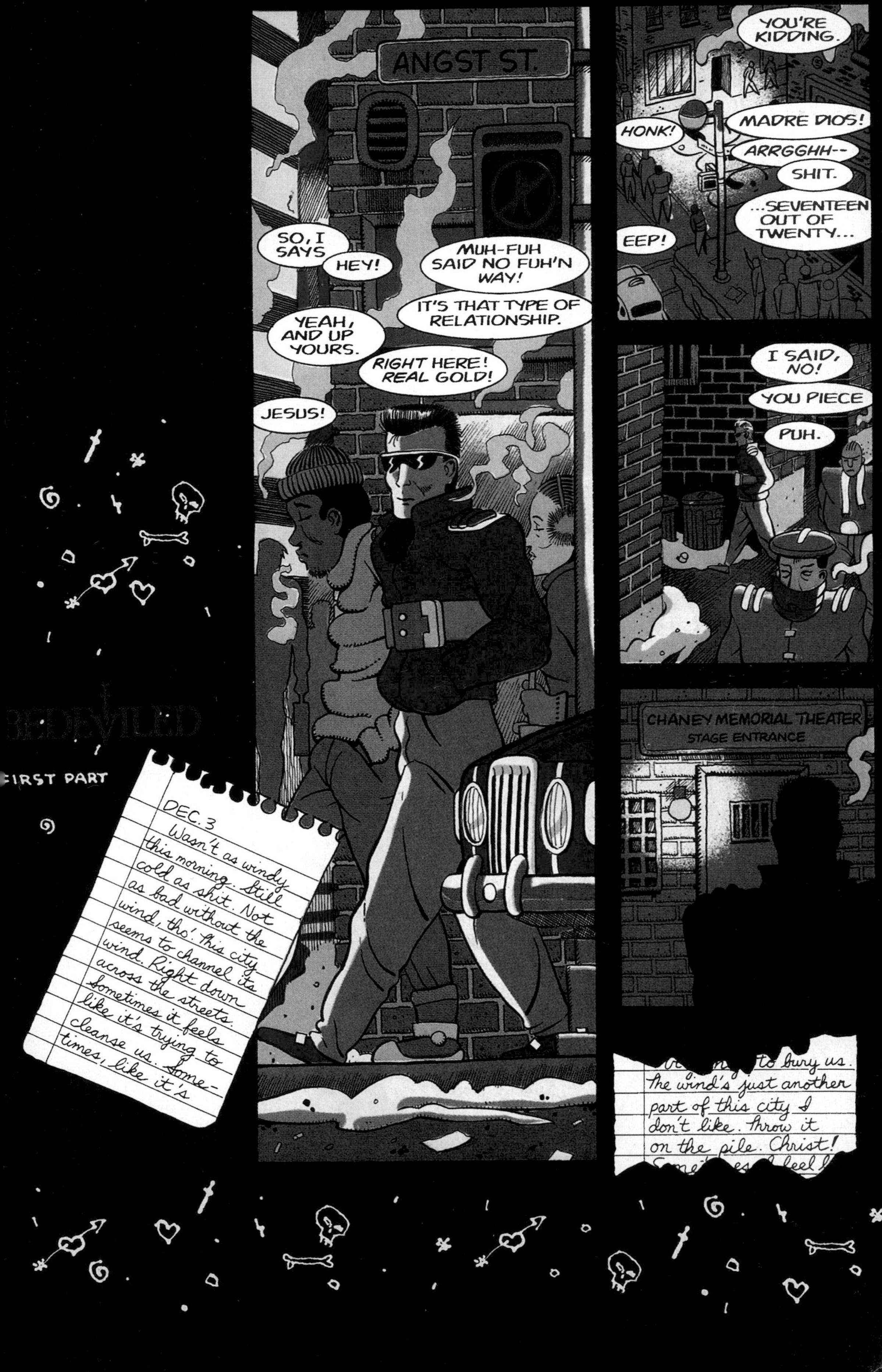

BEDEVILED
IRST PART
ANGST ST.
SO, I SAYS
HEY!
MUH-FUH SAID NO FUH'N WAY!
IT'S THAT TYPE OF RELATIONSHIP.
YEAH, AND UP YOURS.
RIGHT HERE! REAL GOLD!
JESUS!
DEC. 3
Wasn't as windy this morning. Still cold as shit. Not as bad without the wind, tho'. This city seems to channel its wind. Right down across the streets. Sometimes it feels like it's trying to cleanse us. Some-times, like it's
YOU'RE KIDDING.
HONK!
MADRE DIOS!
ARRGGHH--
SHIT.
...SEVENTEEN OUT OF TWENTY...
EEP!
I SAID, NO!
YOU PIECE
PUH.
CHANEY MEMORIAL THEATER
STAGE ENTRANCE
to bury us. The wind's just another part of this city I don't like. Throw it on the pile. Christ!

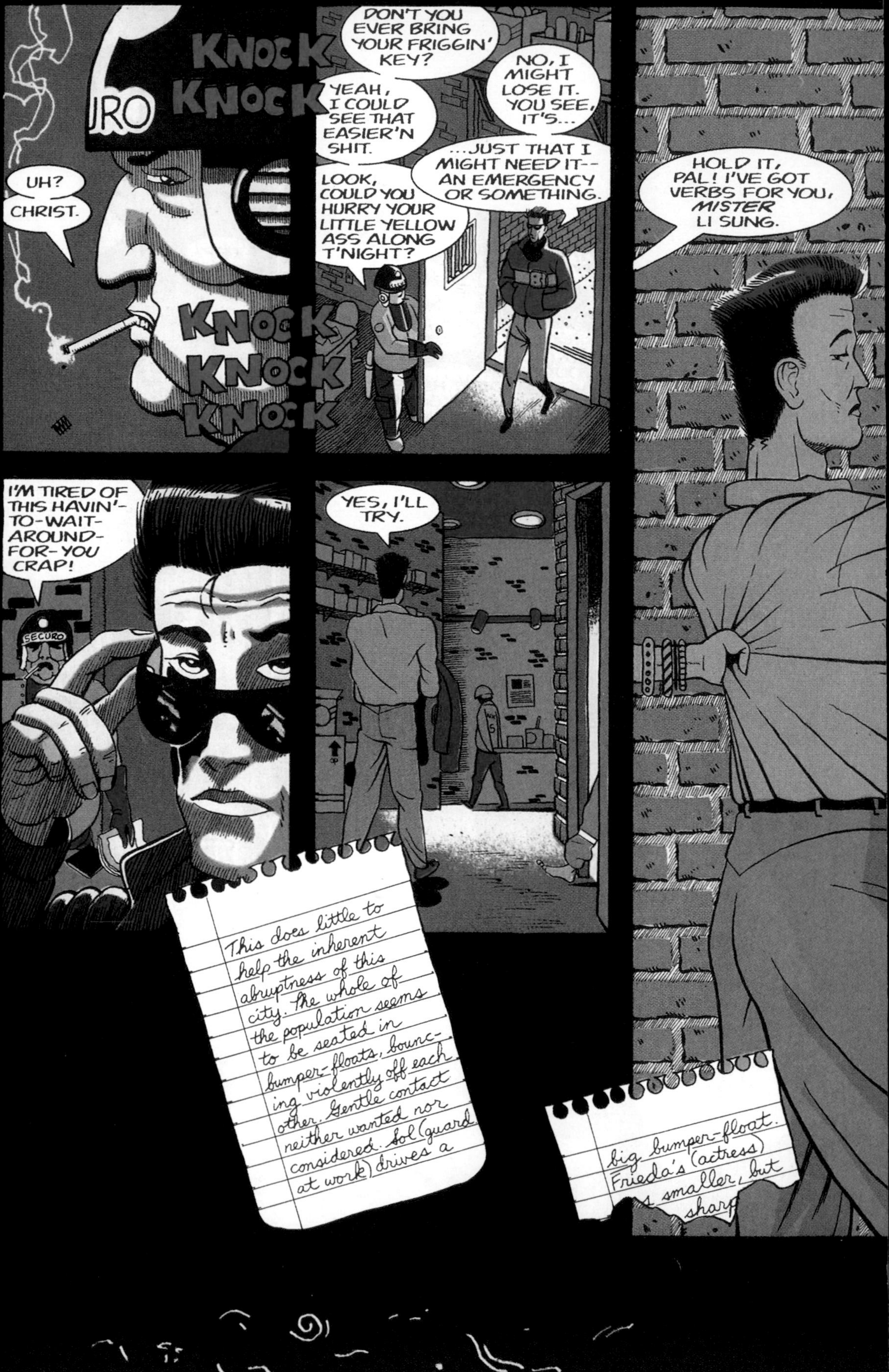
KNOCK KNOCK
UH?
CHRIST.
KNOCK KNOCK KNOCK
DON'T YOU EVER BRING YOUR FRIGGIN' KEY?
NO, I MIGHT LOSE IT. YOU SEE, IT'S...
YEAH, I COULD SEE THAT EASIER'N SHIT.
...JUST THAT I MIGHT NEED IT-- AN EMERGENCY OR SOMETHING.
LOOK, COULD YOU HURRY YOUR LITTLE YELLOW ASS ALONG T'NIGHT?
HOLD IT, PAL! I'VE GOT VERBS FOR YOU, MISTER LI SUNG.
I'M TIRED OF THIS HAVIN'-TO-WAIT-AROUND-FOR-YOU CRAP!
SECURO
YES, I'LL TRY.
This does little to help the inherent abruptness of this city. The whole of the population seems to be seated in bumper-floats, bouncing violently off each other. Gentle contact neither wanted nor considered. Sol (guard at work) drives a
big bumper-float. Frieda's (actress) is smaller, but sharp

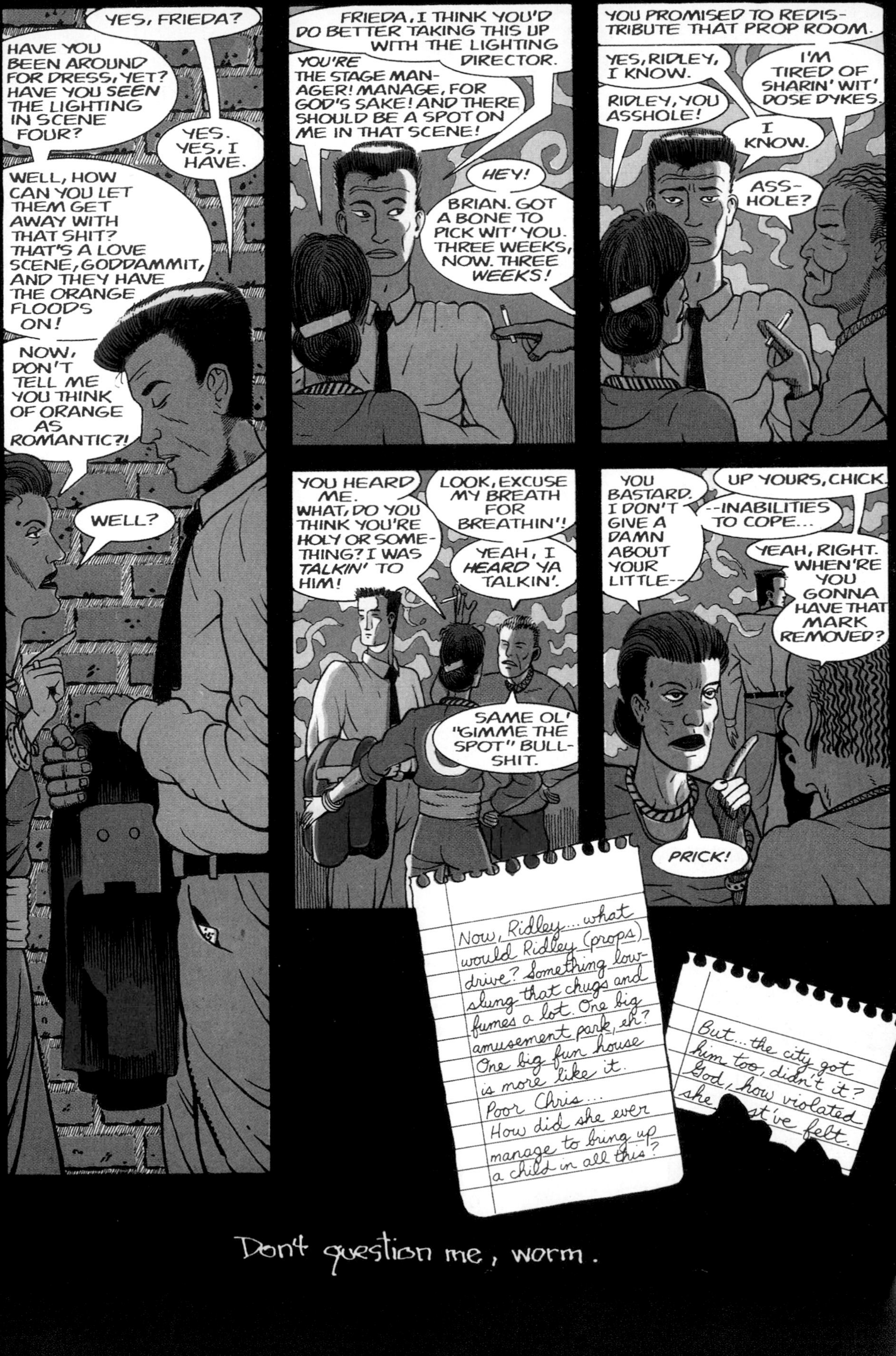
YES, FRIEDA?
HAVE YOU BEEN AROUND FOR DRESS, YET? HAVE YOU SEEN THE LIGHTING IN SCENE FOUR?
YES. YES, I HAVE.
WELL, HOW CAN YOU LET THEM GET AWAY WITH THAT SHIT? THAT'S A LOVE SCENE, GODDAMMIT, AND THEY HAVE THE ORANGE FLOODS ON!
NOW, DON'T TELL ME YOU THINK OF ORANGE AS ROMANTIC?!
WELL?
FRIEDA, I THINK YOU'D DO BETTER TAKING THIS UP WITH THE LIGHTING DIRECTOR.
YOU'RE THE STAGE MANAGER! MANAGE, FOR GOD'S SAKE! AND THERE SHOULD BE A SPOT ON ME IN THAT SCENE!
HEY!
BRIAN. GOT A BONE TO PICK WIT' YOU. THREE WEEKS, NOW. THREE WEEKS!
YOU PROMISED TO REDISTRIBUTE THAT PROP ROOM.
YES, RIDLEY, I KNOW.
I'M TIRED OF SHARIN' WIT' DOSE DYKES.
RIDLEY, YOU ASSHOLE!
I KNOW.
ASSHOLE?
YOU HEARD ME. WHAT, DO YOU THINK YOU'RE HOLY OR SOMETHING? I WAS TALKIN' TO HIM!
LOOK, EXCUSE MY BREATH FOR BREATHIN'!
YEAH, I HEARD YA TALKIN'.
SAME OL' "GIMME THE SPOT" BULLSHIT.
YOU BASTARD. I DON'T GIVE A DAMN ABOUT YOUR LITTLE--
UP YOURS, CHICK.
--INABILITIES TO COPE...
YEAH, RIGHT. WHEN'RE YOU GONNA HAVE THAT MARK REMOVED?
PRICK!
Now, Ridley... what would Ridley (props) drive? Something low-slung that chugs and fumes a lot. One big amusement park, eh? One big fun house is more like it. Poor Chris... How did she ever manage to bring up a child in all this?
But... the city got him too, didn't it? God, how violated she [illegible]st've felt.
Don't question me, worm.

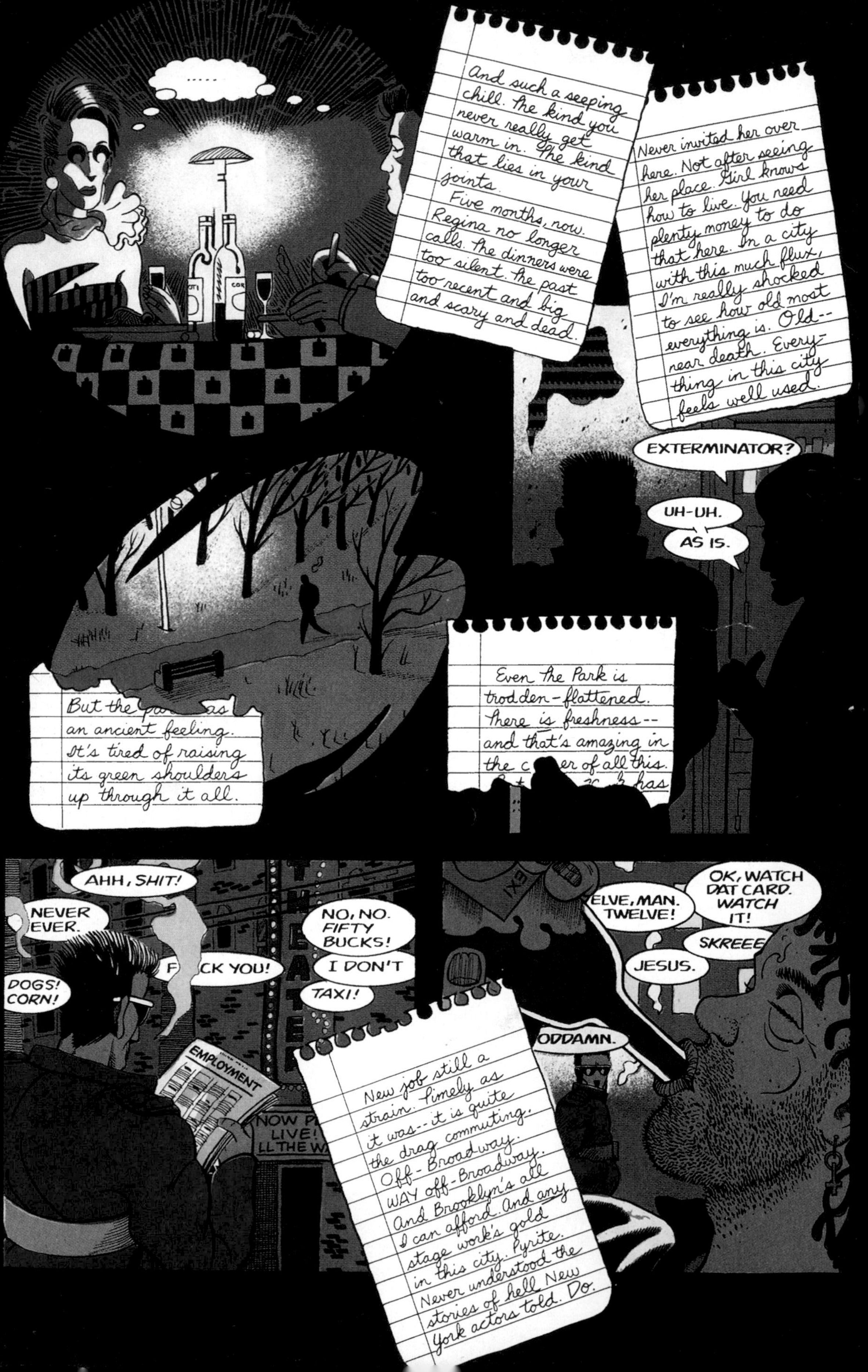
......
And such a seeping chill. The kind you never really get warm in. The kind that lies in your joints.
Five months, now. Regina no longer calls. The dinners were too silent. The past too recent and big and scary and dead.
Never invited her over here. Not after seeing her place. Girl knows how to live. You need plenty money to do that here. In a city with this much flux, I'm really shocked to see how old most everything is. Old--everything is. Old--near death. Everything in this city feels well used.
EXTERMINATOR?
UH-UH.
AS IS.
But the pa as an ancient feeling. It's tired of raising its green shoulders up through it all.
Even the Park is trodden-flattened. There is freshness--and that's amazing in the c er of all this.
has
AHH, SHIT!
NEVER EVER.
NO, NO. FIFTY BUCKS!
F CK YOU!
I DON'T
DOGS! CORN!
TAXI!
EMPLOYMENT
NOW P LIVE! LL THE W
ELVE, MAN. TWELVE!
OK, WATCH DAT CARD. WATCH IT!
SKREEE
JESUS.
ODDAMN.
New job still a strain. Timely as it was--it is quite the drag commuting. Off-Broadway. WAY off-Broadway. And Brooklyn's all I can afford. And any stage work's gold in this city. Pyrite. Never understood the stories of hell New York actors told. Do.

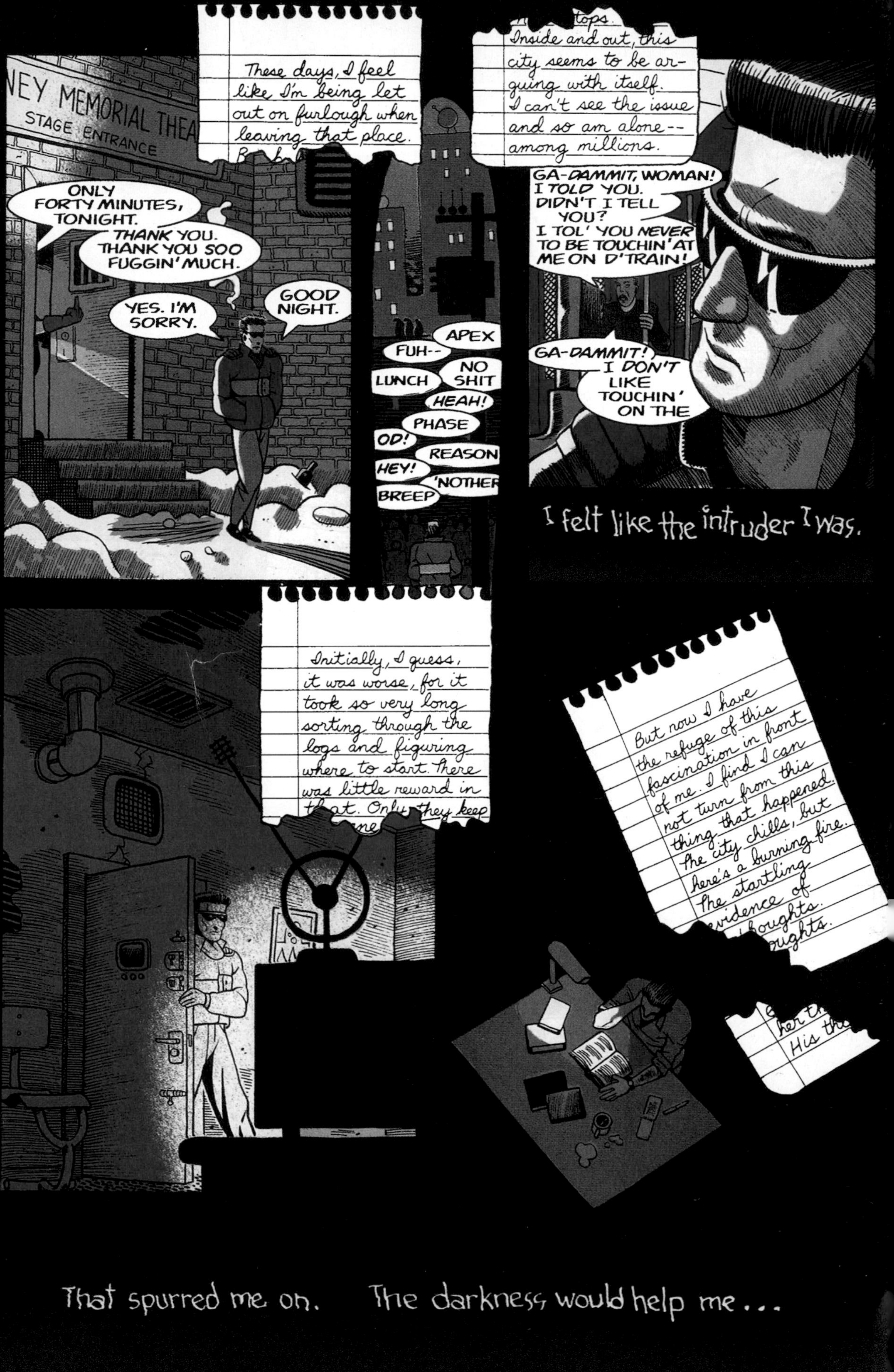
NEY MEMORIAL THEA
STAGE ENTRANCE
These days, I feel like I'm being let out on furlough when leaving that place.
ONLY FORTY MINUTES, TONIGHT.
THANK YOU. THANK YOU SOO FUGGIN' MUCH.
YES. I'M SORRY.
GOOD NIGHT.
APEX
FUH--
NO SHIT
LUNCH
HEAH!
PHASE
OD!
REASON
HEY!
'NOTHER
BREEP
tops. Inside and out, this city seems to be arguing with itself. I can't see the issue and so am alone -- among millions.
GA-DAMMIT, WOMAN! I TOLD YOU. DIDN'T I TELL YOU? I TOL' YOU NEVER TO BE TOUCHIN' AT ME ON D'TRAIN!
GA-DAMMIT! I DON'T LIKE TOUCHIN' ON THE
I felt like the intruder I was.
Initially, I guess, it was worse, for it took so very long sorting through the logs and figuring where to start. There was little reward in that. Only they keep
But now I have the refuge of this fascination in front of me. I find I can not turn from this thing that happened. The city chills, but here's a burning fire. The startling evidence of thoughts. thoughts.
her th
His th
That spurred me on.
The darkness would help me . . .

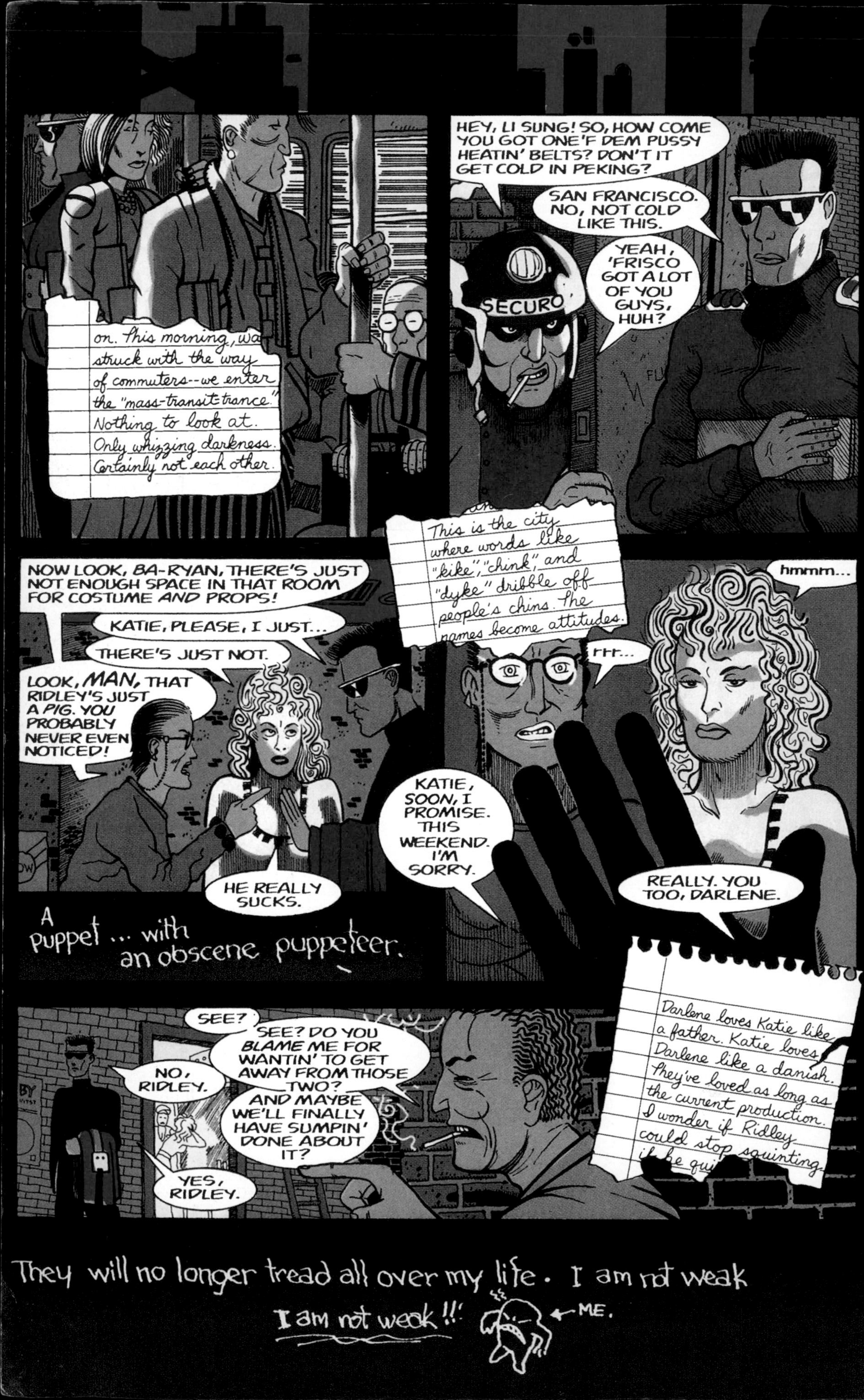
on. This morning, wa
struck with the way
of commuters--we enter
the "mass-transit-trance."
Nothing to look at.
Only whizzing darkness.
Certainly not each other.
HEY, LI SUNG! SO, HOW COME YOU GOT ONE'F DEM PUSSY HEATIN' BELTS? DON'T IT GET COLD IN PEKING?
SAN FRANCISCO. NO, NOT COLD LIKE THIS.
YEAH, 'FRISCO GOT A LOT OF YOU GUYS, HUH?
SECURO
This is the city where words like "kike," "chink," and "dyke" dribble off people's chins. The names become attitudes.
NOW LOOK, BA-RYAN, THERE'S JUST NOT ENOUGH SPACE IN THAT ROOM FOR COSTUME AND PROPS!
KATIE, PLEASE, I JUST...
THERE'S JUST NOT.
LOOK, MAN, THAT RIDLEY'S JUST A PIG. YOU PROBABLY NEVER EVEN NOTICED!
HE REALLY SUCKS.
hmmm...
rrr...
KATIE, SOON, I PROMISE. THIS WEEKEND. I'M SORRY.
REALLY. YOU TOO, DARLENE.
A puppet ... with an obscene puppeteer.
SEE?
SEE? DO YOU BLAME ME FOR WANTIN' TO GET AWAY FROM THOSE TWO? AND MAYBE WE'LL FINALLY HAVE SUMPIN' DONE ABOUT IT?
NO, RIDLEY.
YES, RIDLEY.
Darlene loves Katie like a father. Katie loves Darlene like a danish. They've loved as long as the current production. I wonder if Ridley could stop squinting
They will no longer tread all over my life. I am not weak
I am not weak!!
ME.

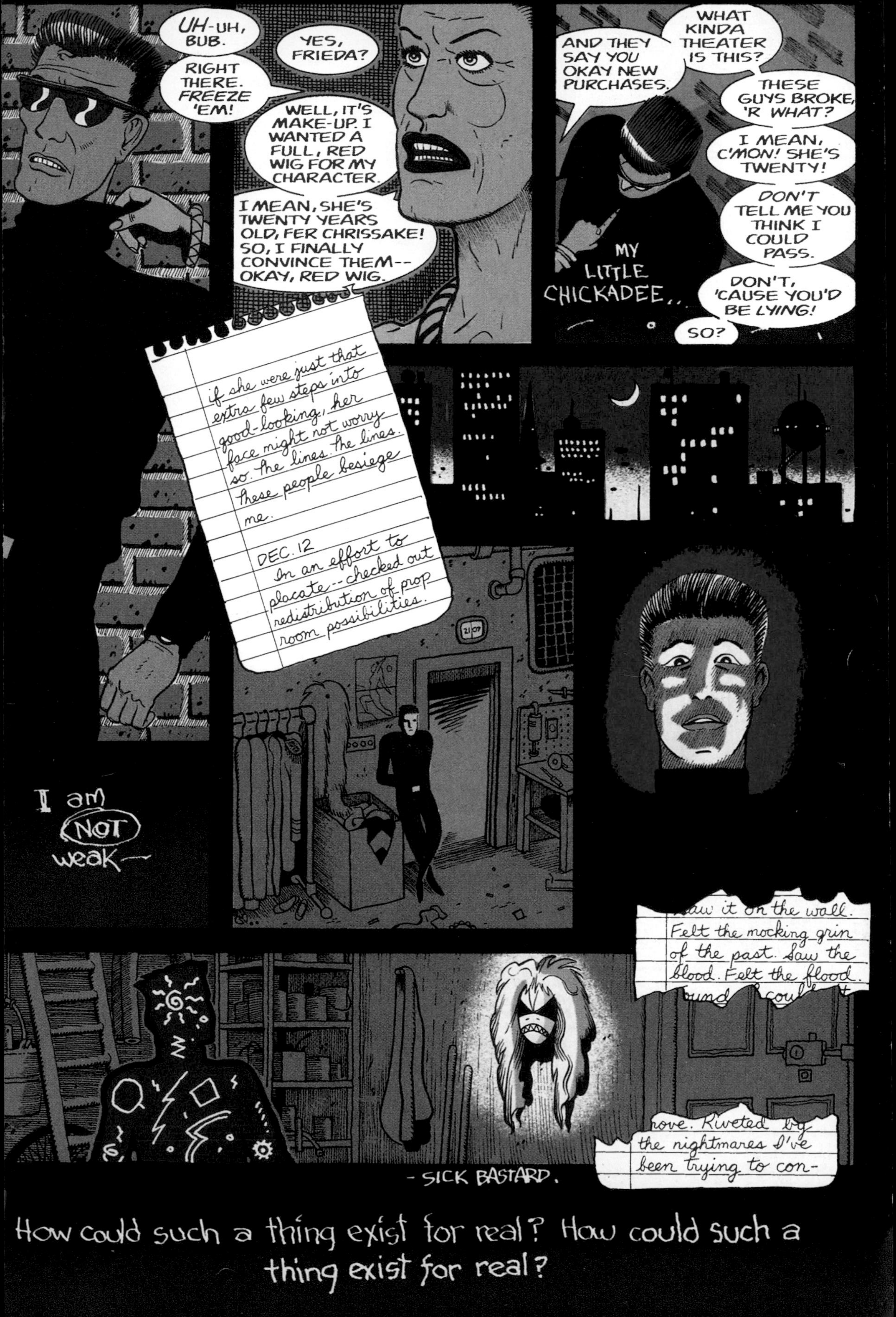
UH-UH, BUB.
RIGHT THERE. FREEZE 'EM!
YES, FRIEDA?
WELL, IT'S MAKE-UP. I WANTED A FULL, RED WIG FOR MY CHARACTER.
I MEAN, SHE'S TWENTY YEARS OLD, FER CHRISSAKE! SO, I FINALLY CONVINCE THEM-- OKAY, RED WIG.
AND THEY SAY YOU OKAY NEW PURCHASES.
WHAT KINDA THEATER IS THIS?
THESE GUYS BROKE, 'R WHAT?
I MEAN, C'MON! SHE'S TWENTY!
DON'T TELL ME YOU THINK I COULD PASS.
MY LITTLE CHICKADEE..
DON'T, 'CAUSE YOU'D BE LYING!
SO?
if she were just that extra few steps into good-looking, her face might not worry so. the lines. the lines. These people besiege me.
DEC. 12
In an effort to placate--checked out redistribution of prop room possibilities.
I am NOT weak—
aw it on the wall. Felt the mocking grin of the past. Saw the blood. Felt the flood.
rove. Riveted by the nightmares I've been trying to con-
- SICK BASTARD.
How could such a thing exist for real? How could such a thing exist for real?

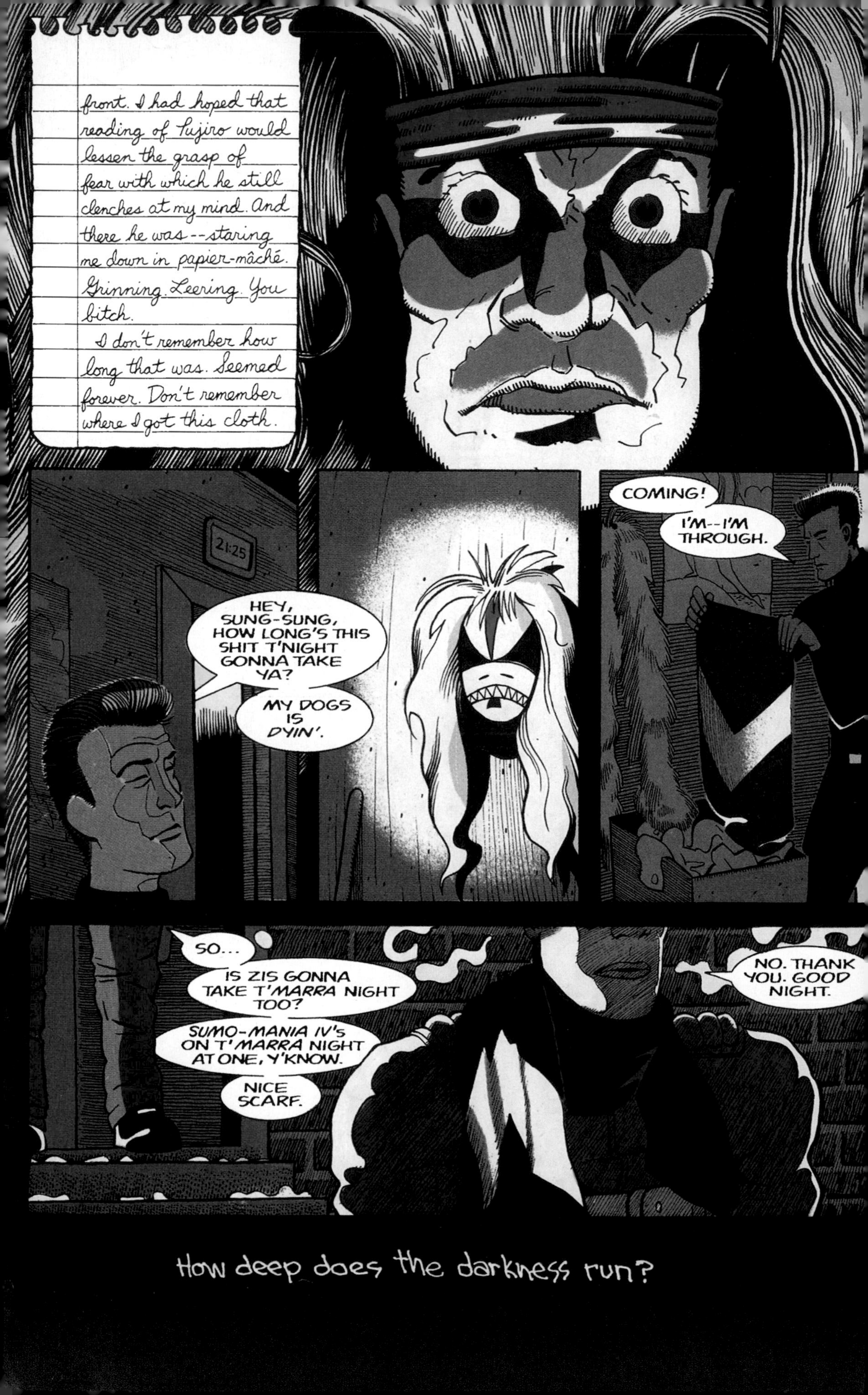
front. I had hoped that reading of Lujiro would lessen the grasp of fear with which he still clenches at my mind. And there he was--staring me down in papier-mâché. Grinning. Leering. You bitch.
I don't remember how long that was. Seemed forever. Don't remember where I got this cloth.
21:25
HEY, SUNG-SUNG, HOW LONG'S THIS SHIT T'NIGHT GONNA TAKE YA?
MY DOGS IS *DYIN'*.
COMING!
I'M--I'M THROUGH.
SO...
IS ZIS GONNA TAKE T'MARRA NIGHT TOO?
SUMO-MANIA IV'S ON T'MARRA NIGHT AT ONE, Y'KNOW.
NICE SCARF.
NO. THANK YOU. GOOD NIGHT.
How deep does the darkness run?

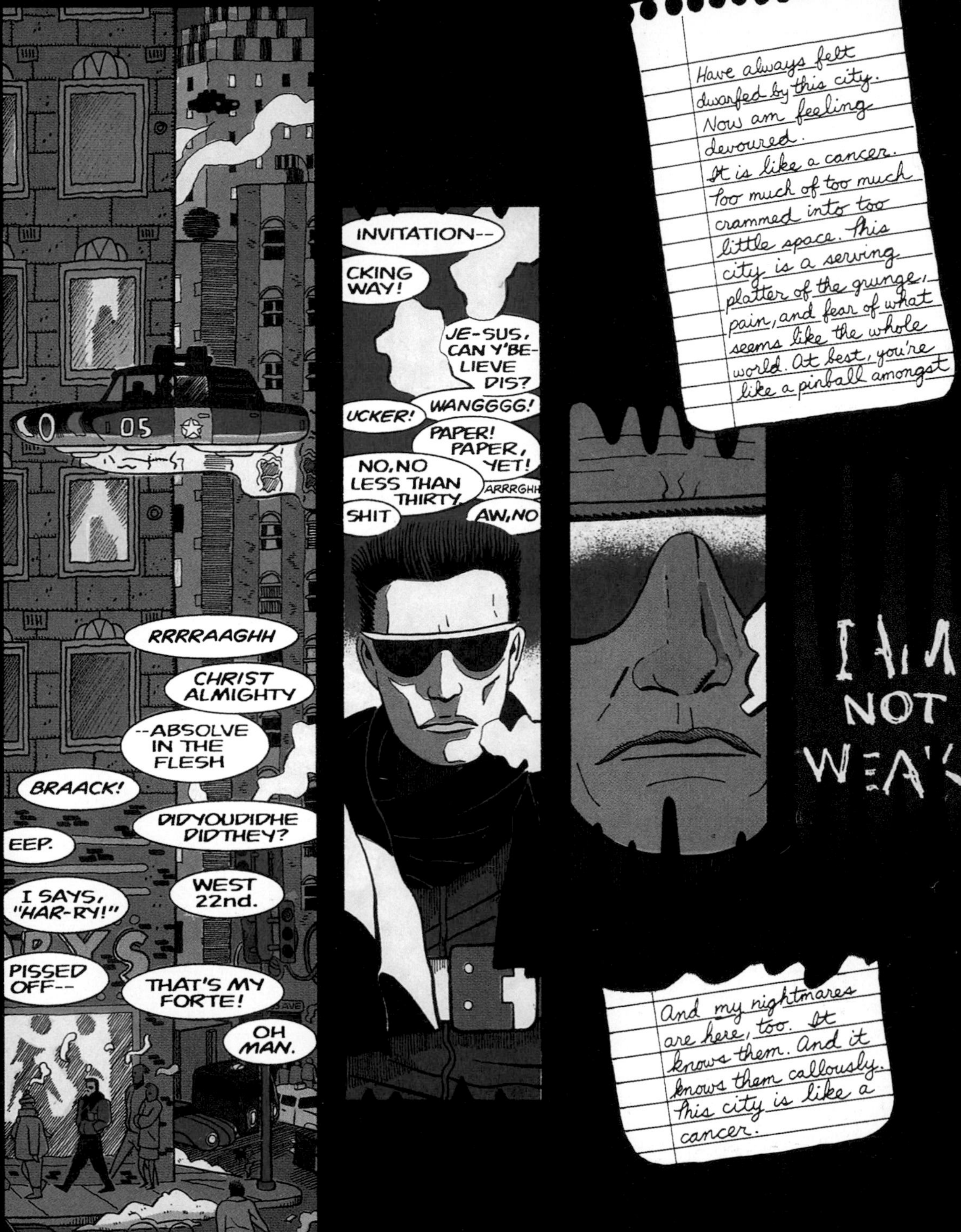
Have always felt dwarfed by this city. Now am feeling devoured. It is like a cancer. Too much of too much crammed into too little space. This city is a serving platter of the grunge, pain, and fear of what seems like the whole world. At best, you're like a pinball amongst
RRRRAAGHH
CHRIST ALMIGHTY
--ABSOLVE IN THE FLESH
BRAACK!
DIDYOUDIDHE DIDTHEY?
EEP.
I SAYS, "HAR-RY!"
WEST 22nd.
PISSED OFF--
THAT'S MY FORTE!
OH MAN.
INVITATION--
CKING WAY!
JE-SUS, CAN Y'BE-LIEVE DIS?
UCKER!
WANGGGG!
PAPER! PAPER, YET!
NO, NO LESS THAN THIRTY
ARRRGHH
SHIT
AW, NO
I AM NOT WEAK
And my nightmares are here, too. It knows them. And it knows them callously. This city is like a cancer.

Hunter knew how to make himself his deadliest-
I am desperate but not hopeless.

How deep does the darkness run? How deep does the darkness run? How deep does the darkness run? How deep does the darkness run? How deep does the darkness run? How
There's an entry wherein Chris talks about how her attitude towards Tu-jiro quickly deteriorated. Everything deteriorates. Not
fear. I remember next to nothing of the trip home. And still don't know where I got this cloth.

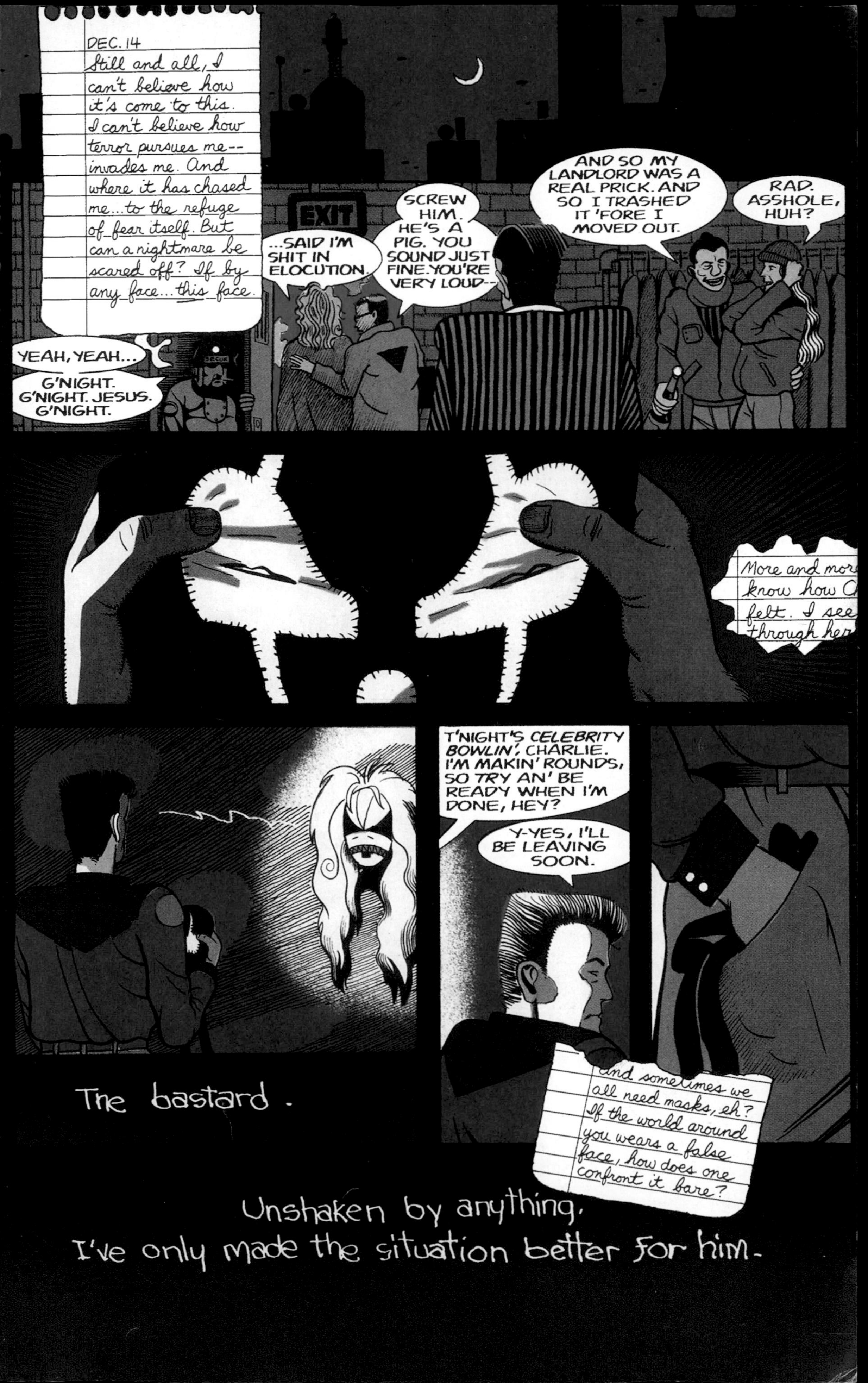
DEC. 14
Still and all, I can't believe how it's come to this. I can't believe how terror pursues me-- invades me. And where it has chased me... to the refuge of fear itself. But can a nightmare be scared off? If by any face... this face.
YEAH, YEAH...
G'NIGHT. G'NIGHT. JESUS. G'NIGHT.
EXIT
...SAID I'M SHIT IN ELOCUTION.
SCREW HIM. HE'S A PIG. YOU SOUND JUST FINE. YOU'RE VERY LOUD--
AND SO MY LANDLORD WAS A REAL PRICK. AND SO I TRASHED IT 'FORE I MOVED OUT.
RAD. ASSHOLE, HUH?
T'NIGHT'S CELEBRITY BOWLIN', CHARLIE. I'M MAKIN' ROUNDS, SO TRY AN' BE READY WHEN I'M DONE, HEY?
Y-YES, I'LL BE LEAVING SOON.
The bastard.
And sometimes we all need masks, eh? If the world around you wears a false face, how does one confront it bare?
Unshaken by anything.
I've only made the situation better for him.

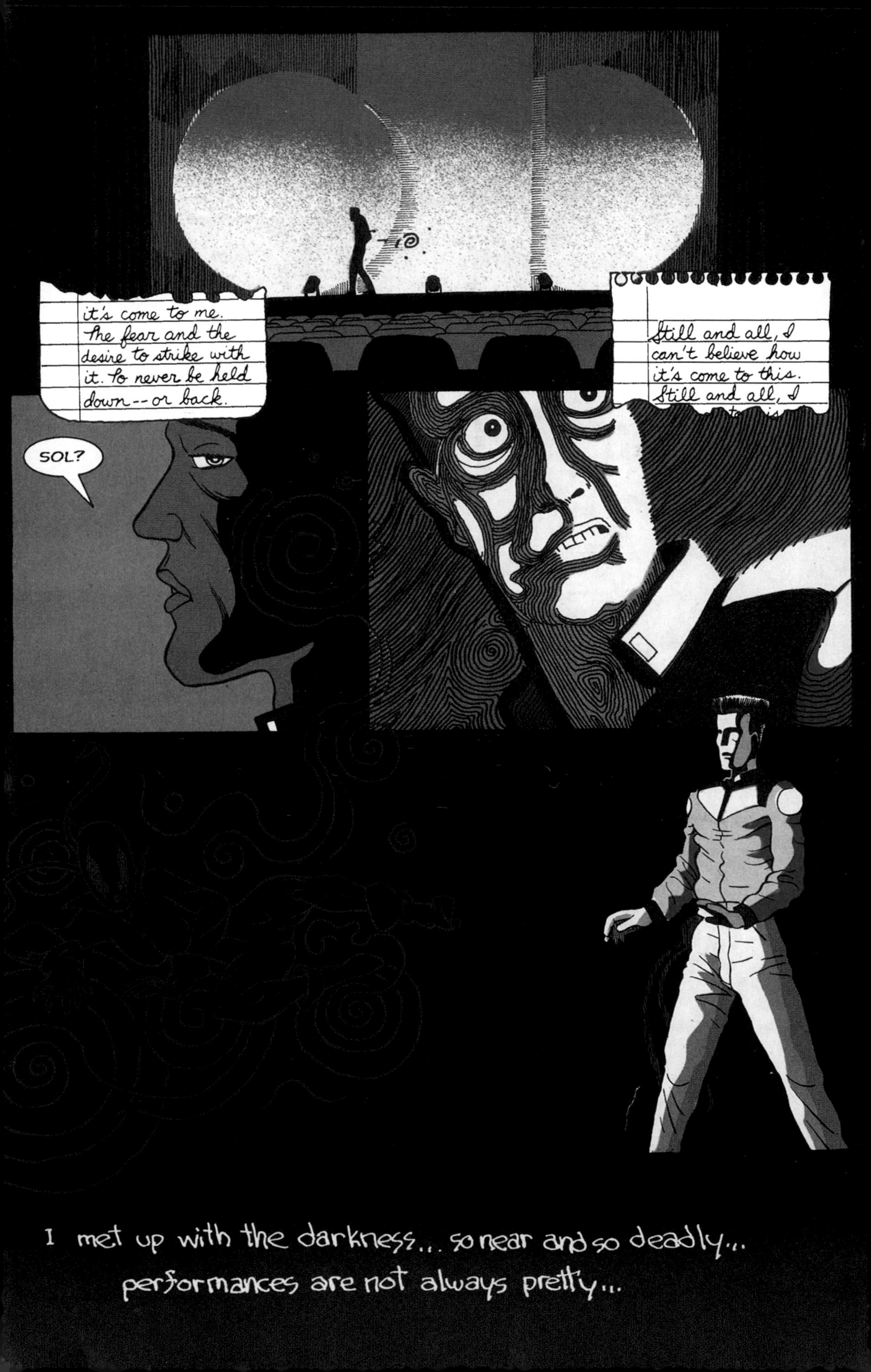
it's come to me. The fear and the desire to strike with it. To never be held down--or back.
Still and all, I can't believe how it's come to this. Still and all, I
SOL?
I met up with the darkness... so near and so deadly...
performances are not always pretty...

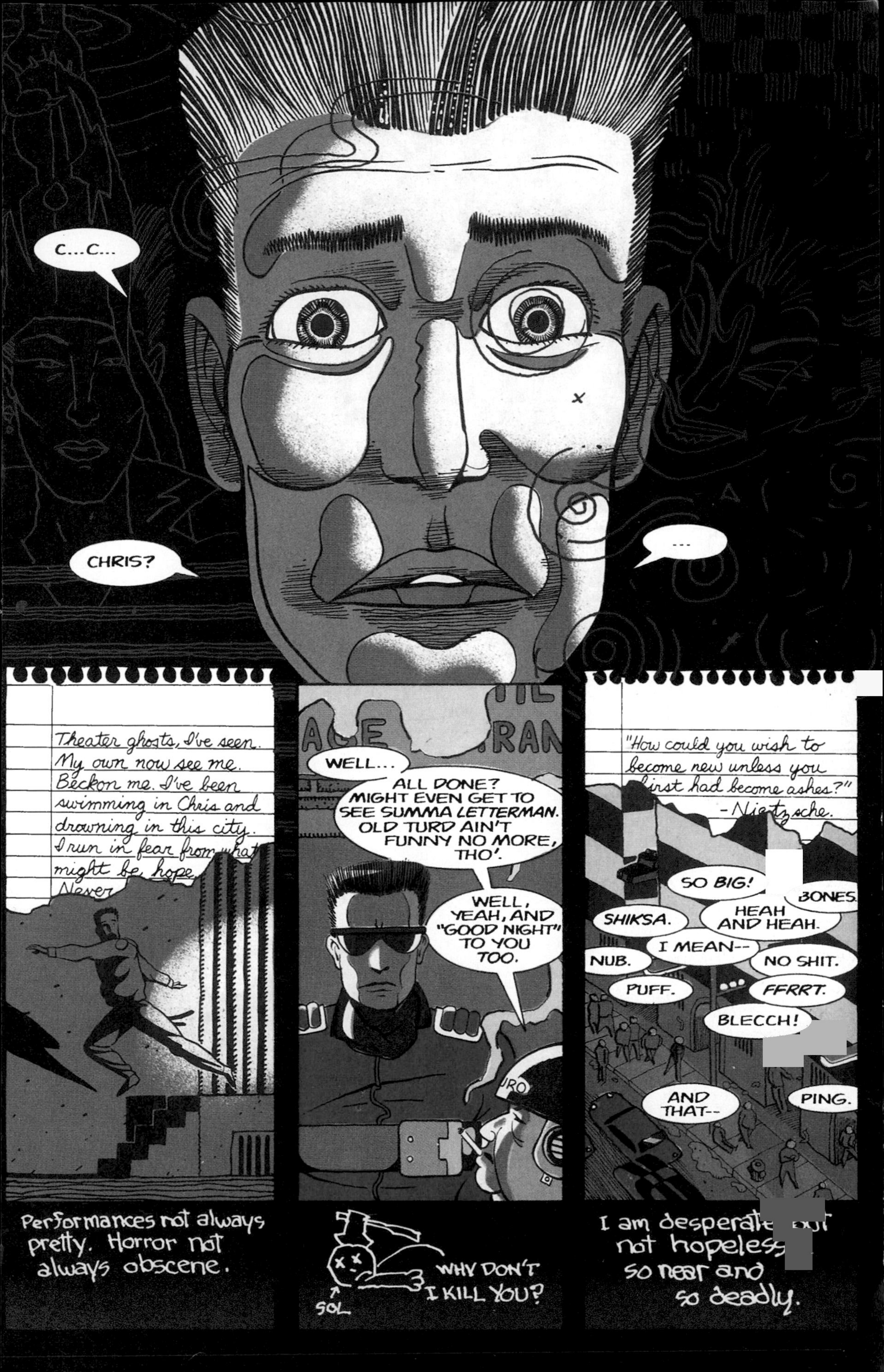

C...C...
CHRIS?
...
Theater ghosts, I've seen. My own now see me. Beckon me. I've been swimming in Chris and drowning in this city. I run in fear from what might be hope. Never
Performances not always pretty. Horror not always obscene.
WELL...
ALL DONE? MIGHT EVEN GET TO SEE SUMMA LETTERMAN. OLD TURD AIN'T FUNNY NO MORE, THO'.
WELL, YEAH, AND "GOOD NIGHT" TO YOU TOO.
SOL
WHY DON'T I KILL YOU?
"How could you wish to become new unless you first had become ashes?" -Nietzsche.
SO BIG!
BONES.
SHIKSA.
HEAH AND HEAH.
I MEAN--
NUB.
NO SHIT.
PUFF.
FFRRT.
BLECCH!
AND THAT--
PING.
I am desperat
not hopeles
so near and
so deadly.

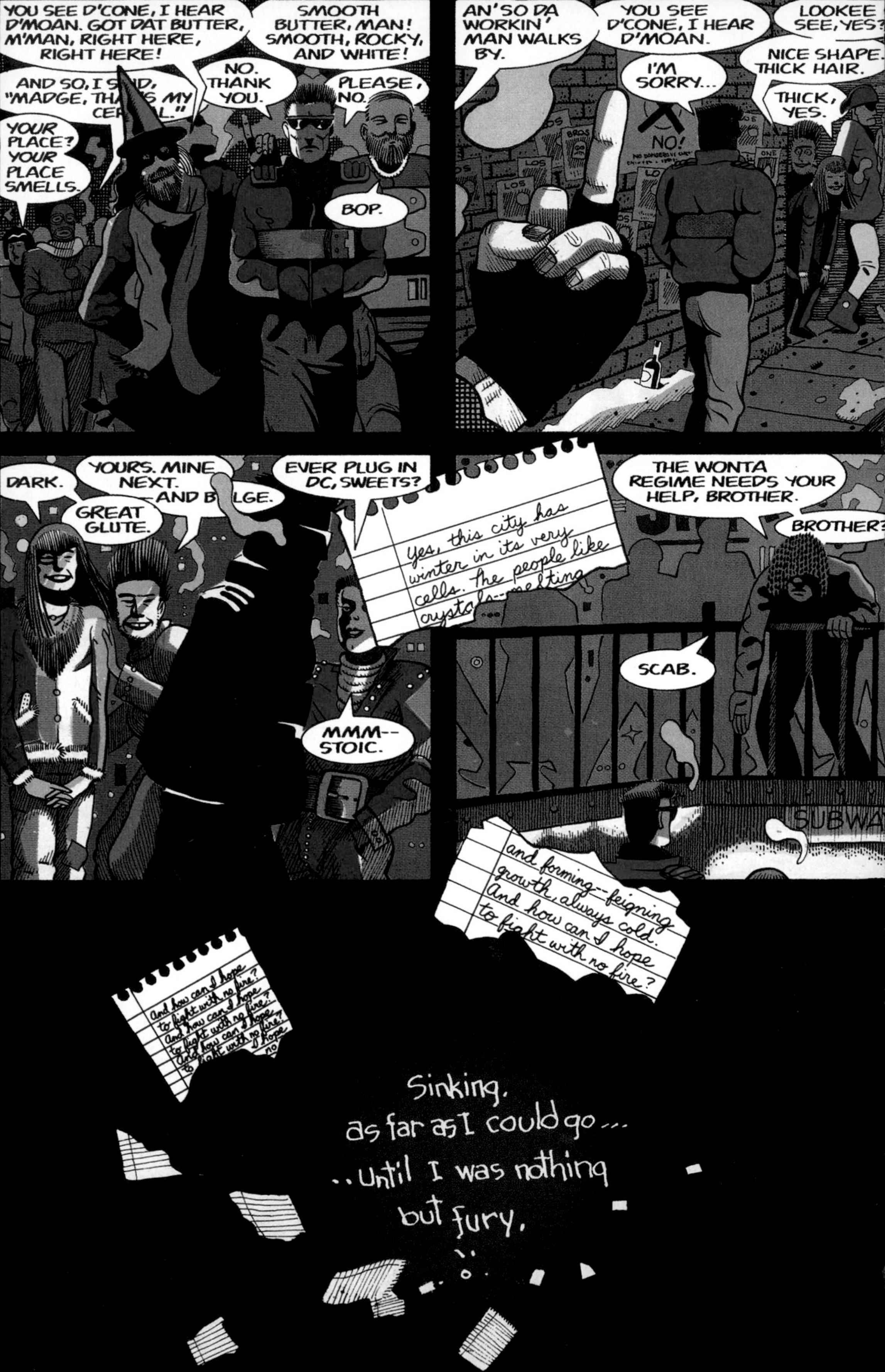
YOU SEE D'CONE, I HEAR D'MOAN. GOT DAT BUTTER, M'MAN, RIGHT HERE, RIGHT HERE!
SMOOTH BUTTER, MAN! SMOOTH, ROCKY, AND WHITE!
AND SO, I SAID, "MADGE, THAT'S MY CEREAL."
NO. THANK YOU.
PLEASE, NO.
YOUR PLACE? YOUR PLACE SMELLS.
BOP.
AN'SO DA WORKIN' MAN WALKS BY.
YOU SEE D'CONE, I HEAR D'MOAN.
LOOKEE SEE, YES?
I'M SORRY...
NICE SHAPE. THICK HAIR.
THICK, YES.
NO!
DARK.
YOURS. MINE NEXT. --AND BULGE.
GREAT GLUTE.
EVER PLUG IN DC, SWEETS?
Yes, this city has winter in its very cells. the people like crystals--melting
MMM-- STOIC.
THE WONTA REGIME NEEDS YOUR HELP, BROTHER.
BROTHER?
SCAB.
SUBWA
and forming--feigning growth, always cold. And how can I hope to fight with no fire?
And how can I hope to fight with no fire? And how can I hope to fight with no fire? And how can I hope to fight with no fire? And how can I hope no
Sinking.
as far as I could go...
..until I was nothing
but fury.

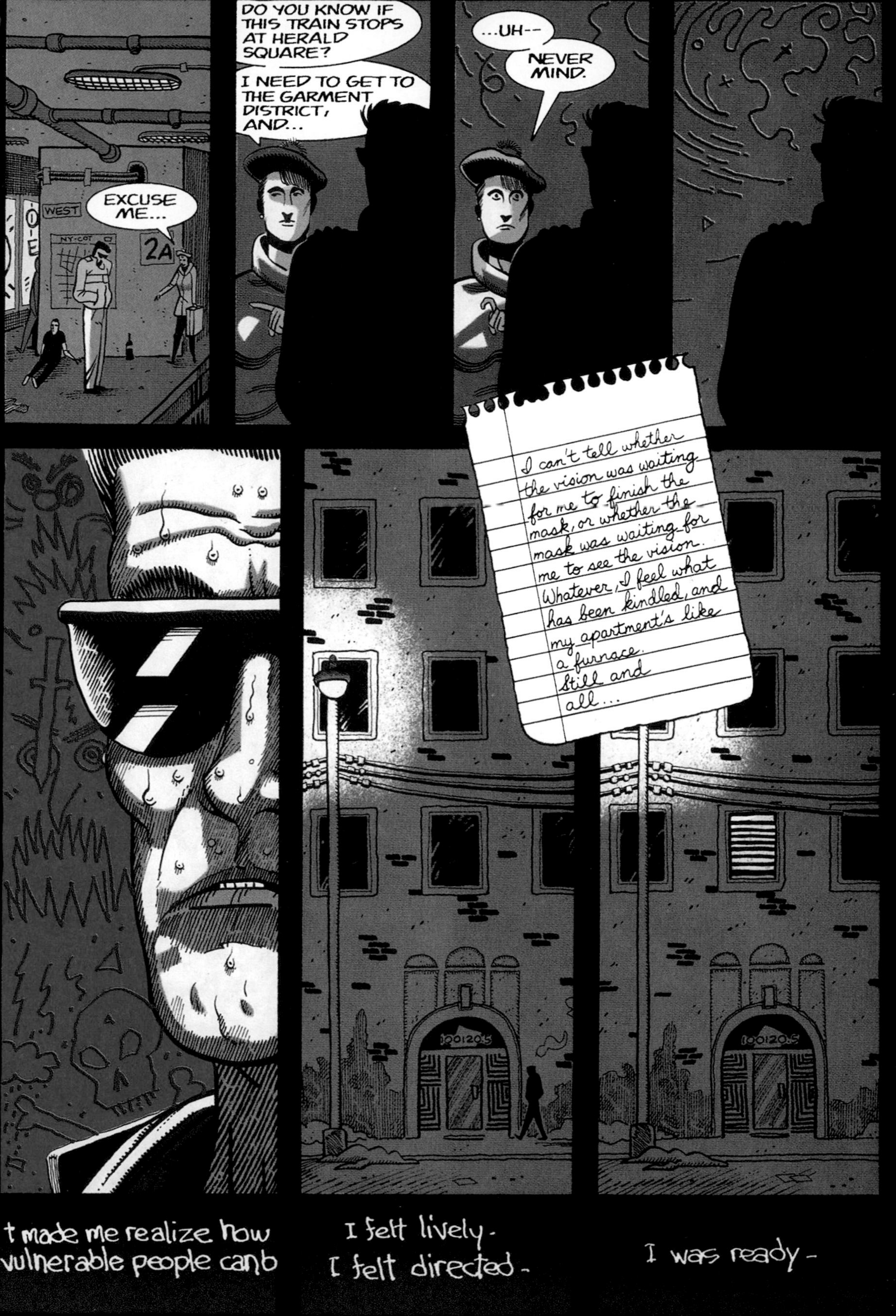
WEST
2A
EXCUSE ME...
DO YOU KNOW IF THIS TRAIN STOPS AT HERALD SQUARE?
I NEED TO GET TO THE GARMENT DISTRICT, AND...
...UH--
NEVER MIND.
I can't tell whether the vision was waiting for me to finish the mask, or whether the mask was waiting for me to see the vision. Whatever, I feel what has been kindled, and my apartment's like a furnace. Still and all...
t made me realize how vulnerable people canb
I felt lively-
I felt directed-
I was ready-

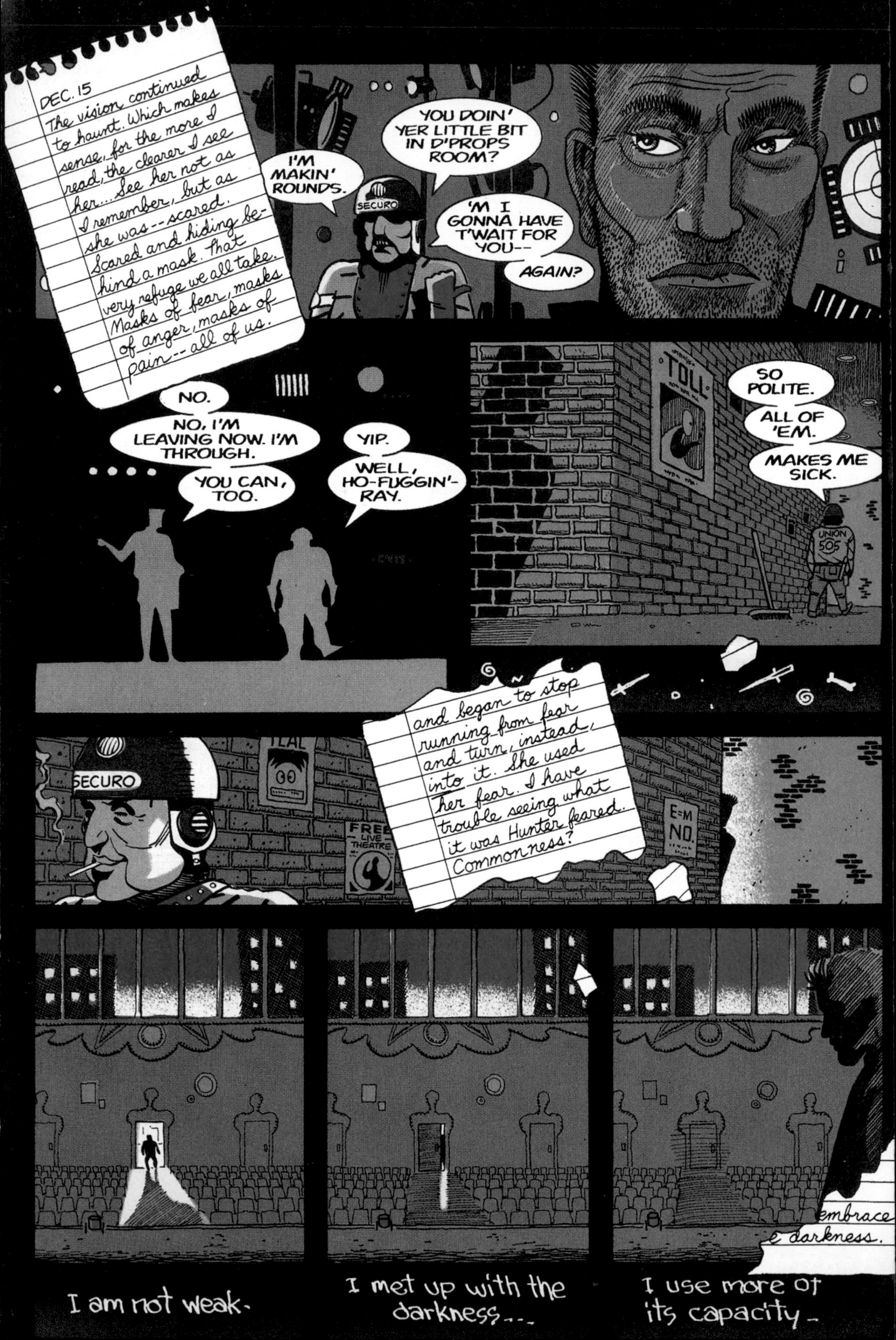
DEC. 15
The vision continued
to haunt. Which makes
sense, for the more I
read, the clearer I see
her... See her not as
I remember, but as
she was--scared.
Scared and hiding be-
hind a mask. That
very refuge we all take.
Masks of fear, masks
of anger, masks of
pain--all of us.
YOU DOIN' YER LITTLE BIT IN D'PROPS ROOM?
I'M MAKIN' ROUNDS.
SECURO
'M I GONNA HAVE T'WAIT FOR YOU--
AGAIN?
NO.
NO, I'M LEAVING NOW. I'M THROUGH.
YOU CAN, TOO.
YIP.
WELL, HO-FUGGIN'-RAY.
TOLL
SO POLITE.
ALL OF 'EM.
MAKES ME SICK.
UNION 505
and began to stop
running from fear
and turn, instead,
into it. She used
her fear. I have
trouble seeing what
it was Hunter feared.
Commonness?
SECURO
FREE LIVE THEATRE
E=M NO.
embrace
e darkness.
I am not weak.
I met up with the darkness...
I use more of its capacity.

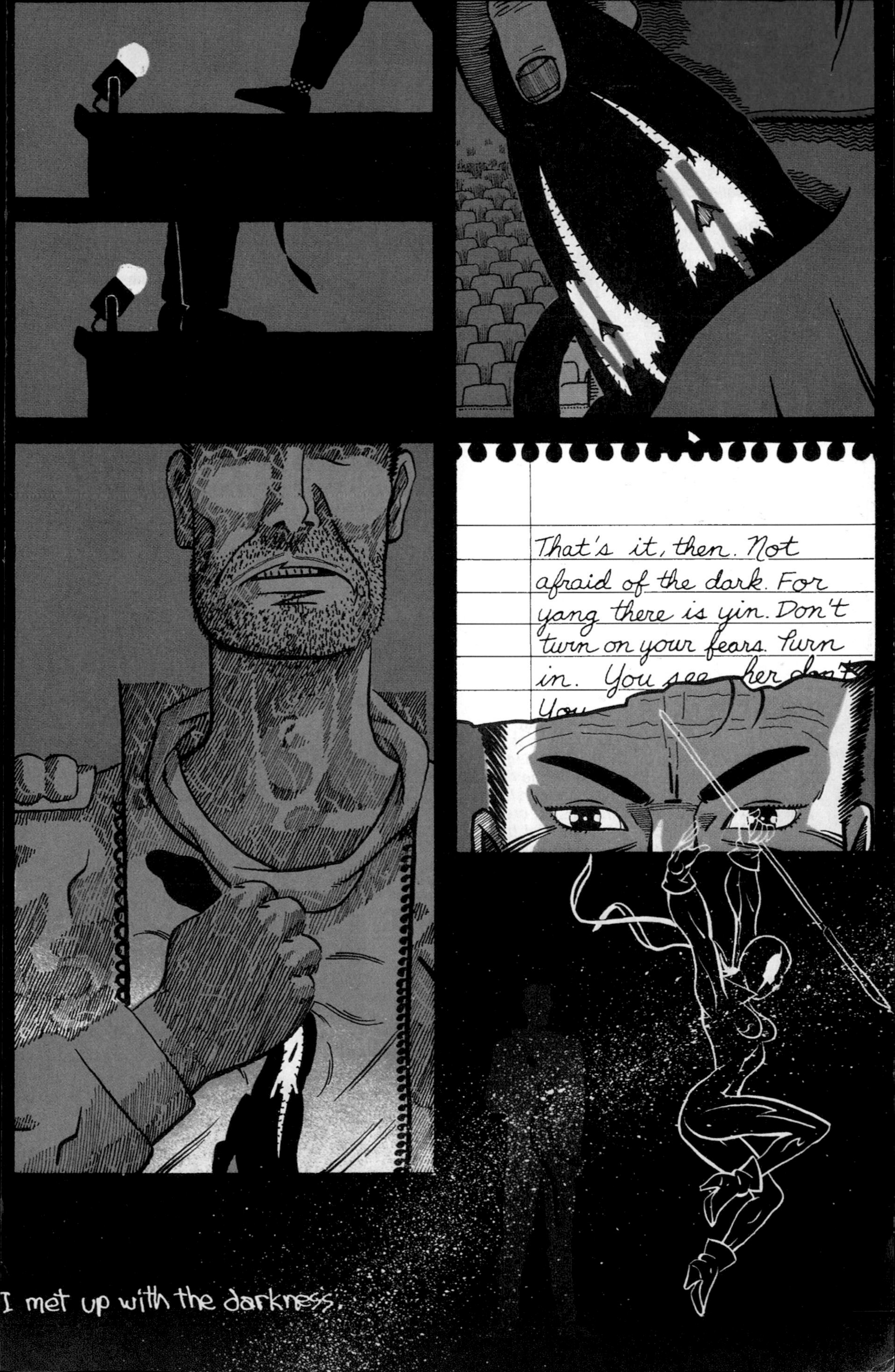
That's it, then. Not afraid of the dark. For yang there is yin. Don't turn on your fears. Turn in. You see her
I met up with the darkness.

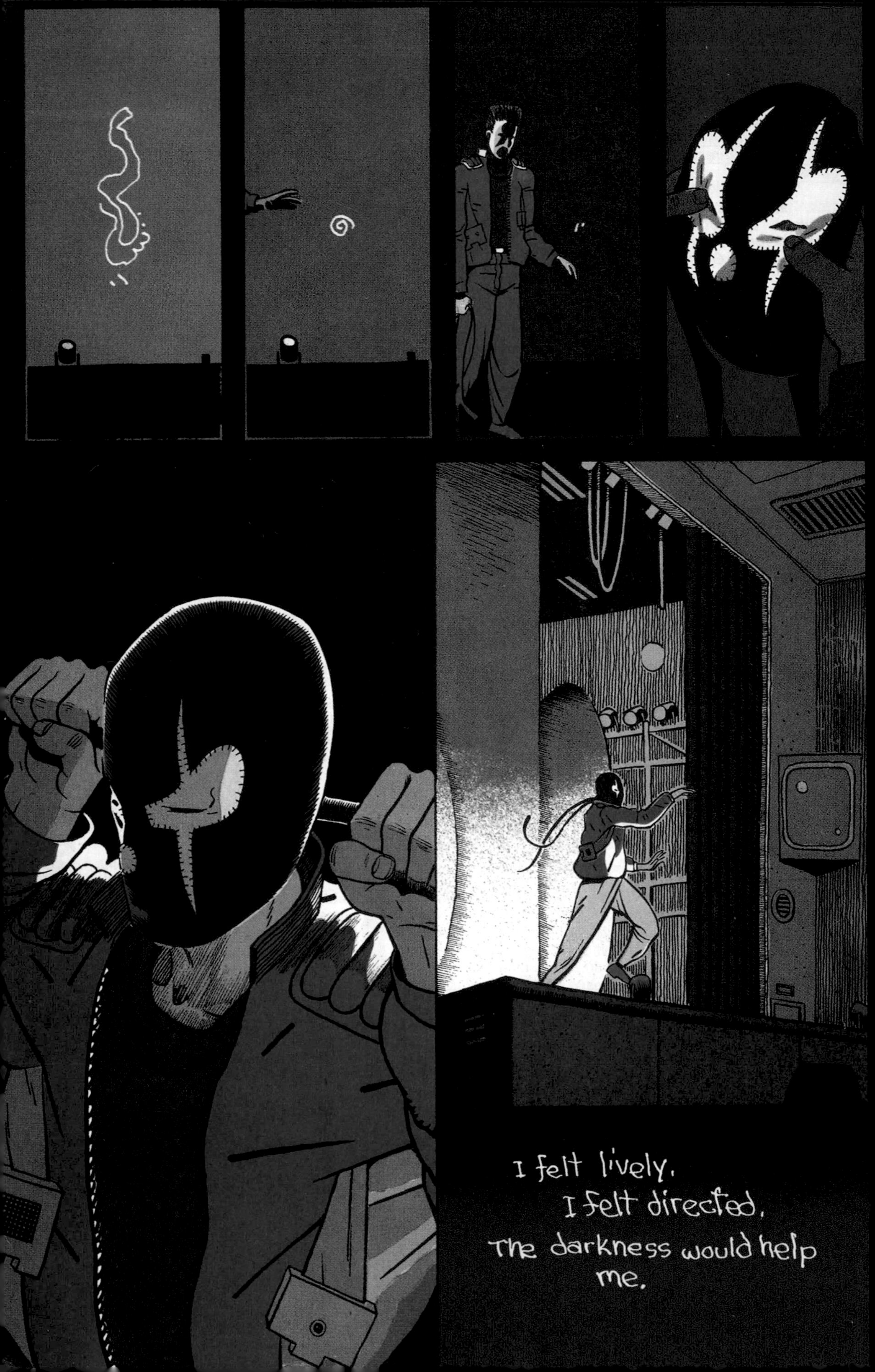
I felt lively.
I felt directed.
The darkness would help me.

LI SUNG?

IS ZAT YOU? WHOZARE?

ARRIGHT, GODDAMMIT! I HAD ENOUGH O' DIS SHIT! C'MON OUT!

HEY! WHOZARE?!

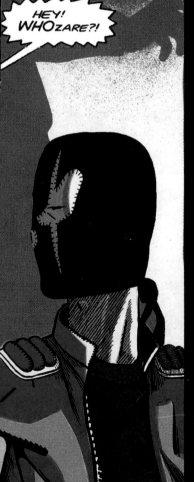

I KNOW SOMEONE'S HERE!

COME OUT AND NO BULLSHIT!

I MEAN IT--DON'T MAKE ME BUST YER ASS!

UNION 505

He's the one who's nervous--

who's scared...

GRUMBLE... GRRUFFFF...

...rrrr...

SECURO

SECURO

SECURO

I AM STRONG

He is abrasive in nearly every way.

Repulsive.

Brutal.

He's disgusting.

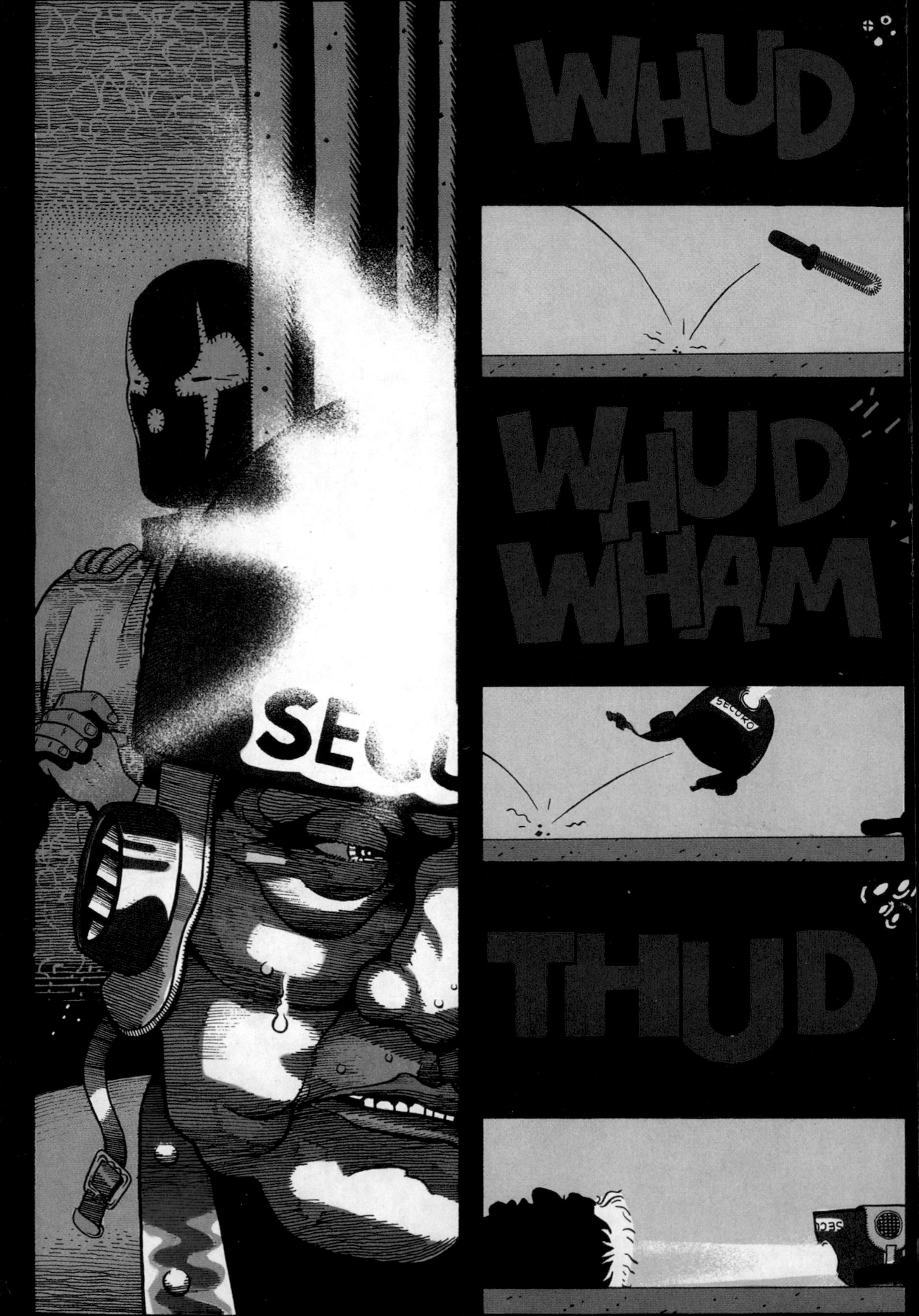
WHUD
SECURO
WHUD
WHAM
SECURO
THUD
SECU

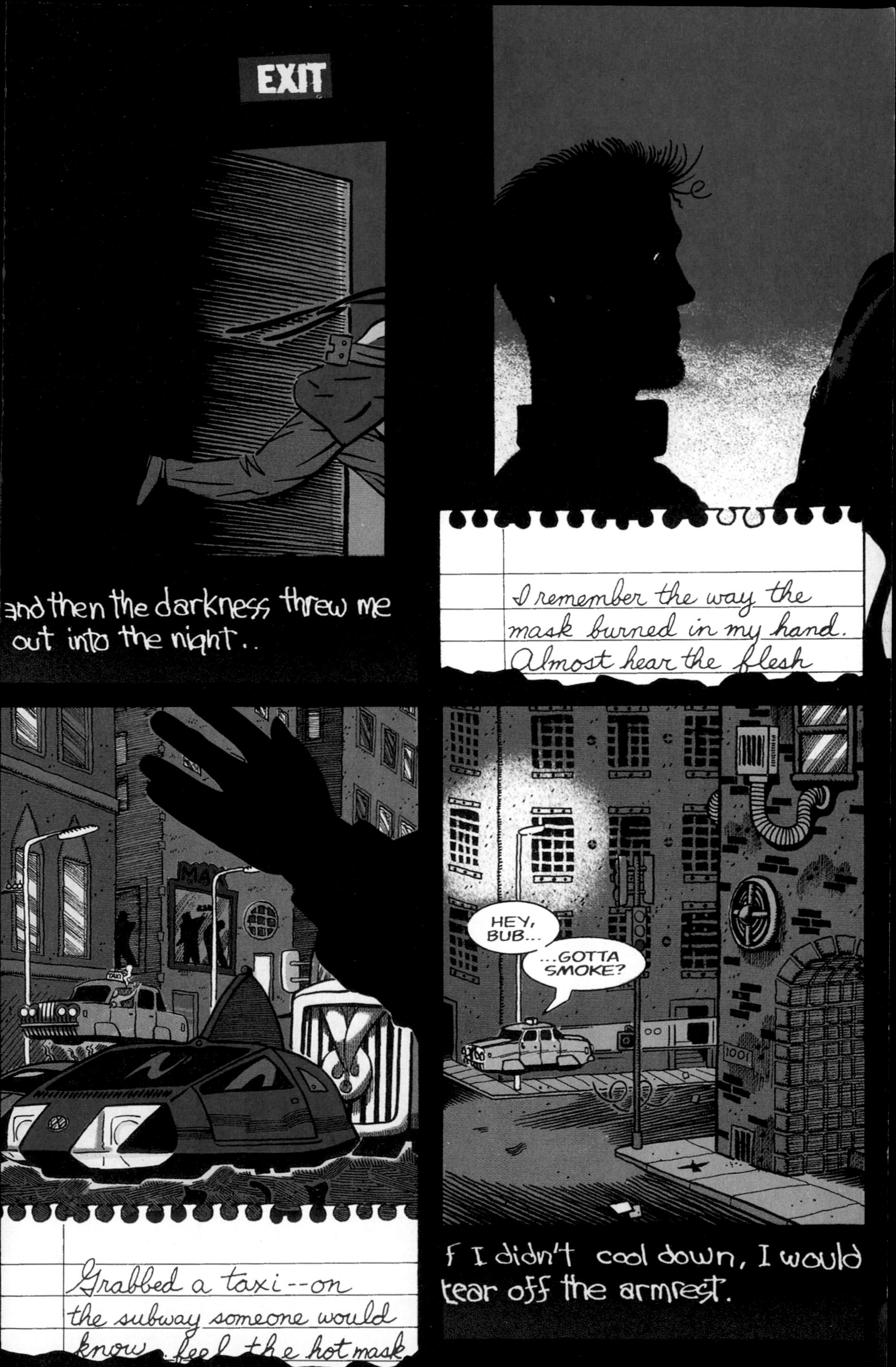
EXIT
and then the darkness threw me
out into the night..
I remember the way the
mask burned in my hand.
Almost hear the flesh
Grabbed a taxi--on
the subway someone would
know..feel the hot mask
HEY, BUB...
...GOTTA SMOKE?
f I didn't cool down, I would
tear off the armrest.

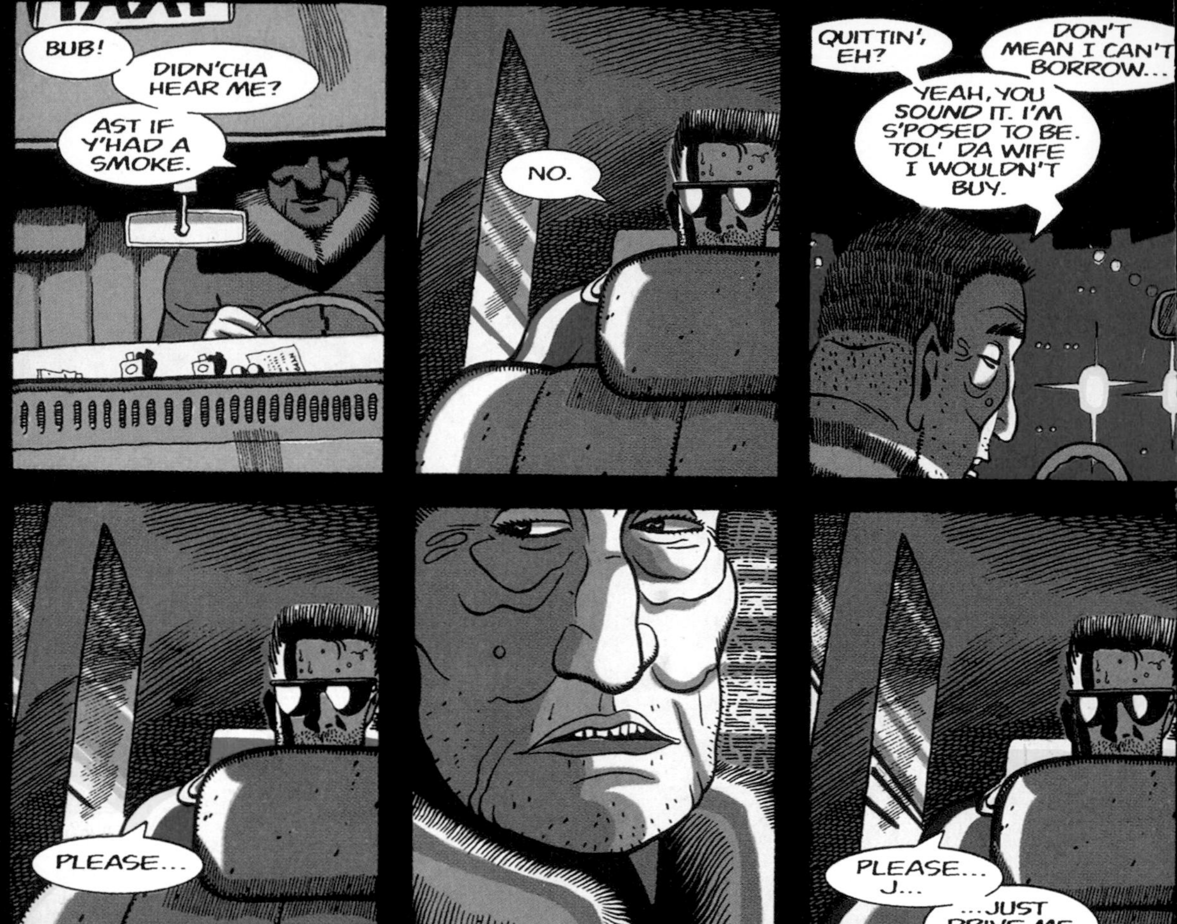
BUB!
DIDN'CHA HEAR ME?
AST IF Y'HAD A SMOKE.
NO.
QUITTIN', EH?
YEAH, YOU SOUND IT. I'M S'POSED TO BE. TOL' DA WIFE I WOULDN'T BUY.
DON'T MEAN I CAN'T BORROW...
PLEASE...
PLEASE... J...
...JUST DRIVE ME. QUICKLY.
S
REST
NORAD

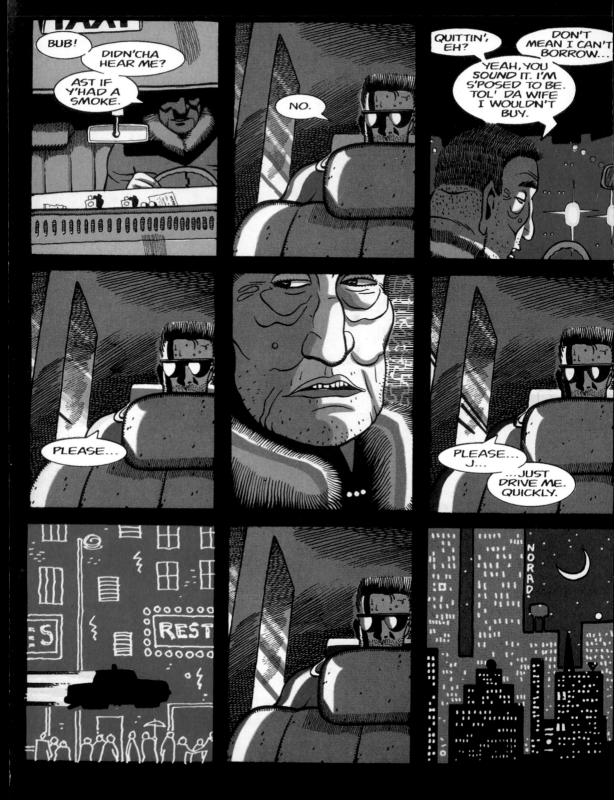

I am seething and single-minded. He's so very lucky he isn't dead.

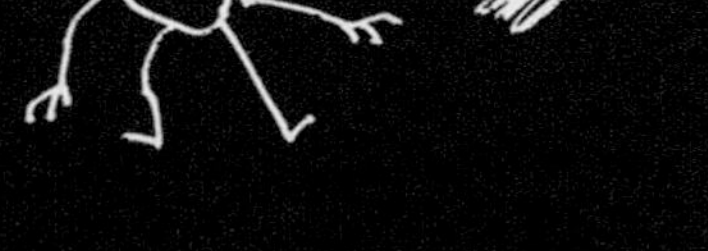
Dead.

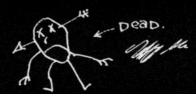

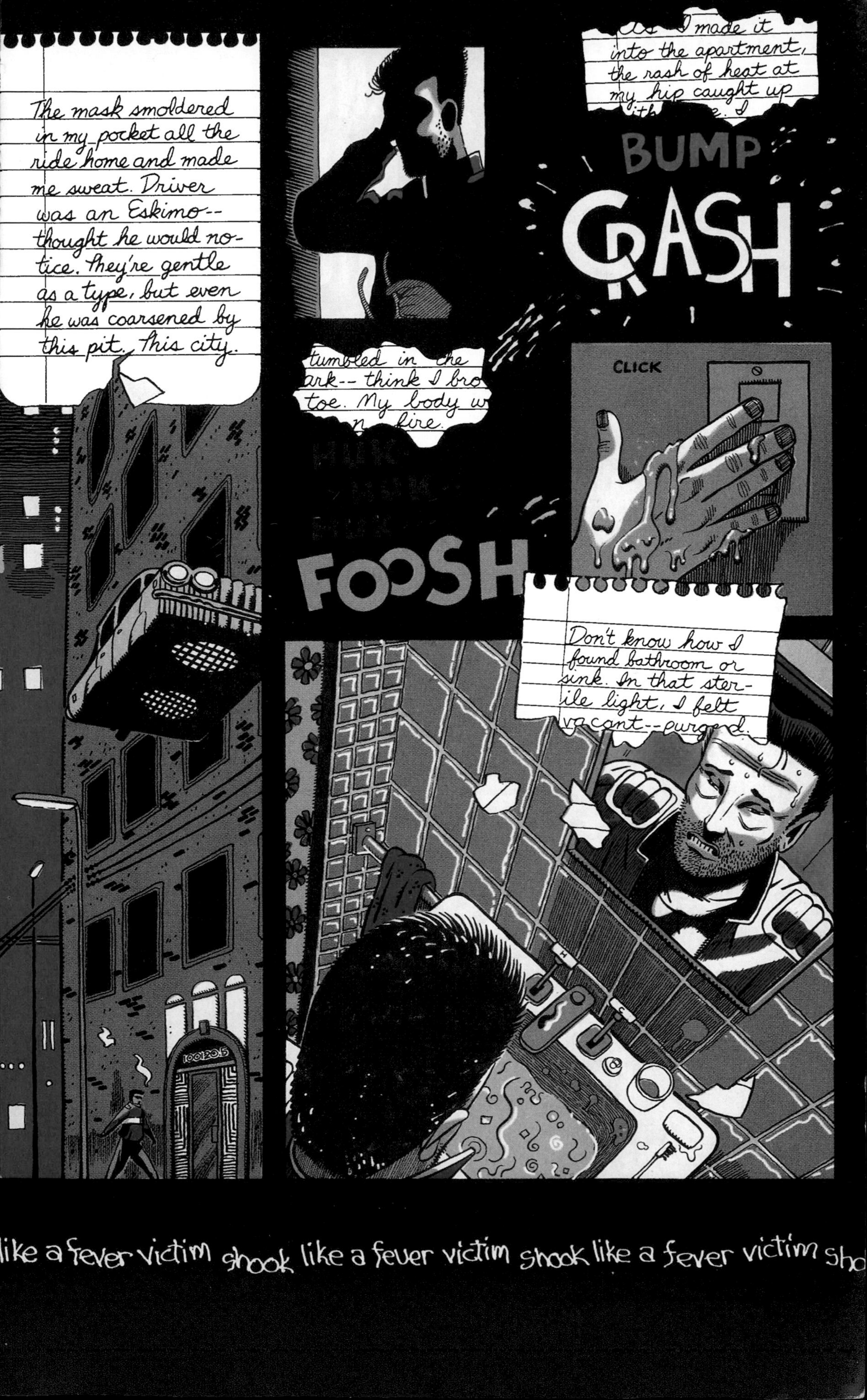

The mask smoldered in my pocket all the ride home and made me sweat. Driver was an Eskimo-- thought he would notice. They're gentle as a type, but even he was coarsened by this pit. This city.
As I made it into the apartment, the rash of heat at my hip caught up
BUMP
CRASH
tumbled in the ark-- think I bro toe. My body w n fire.
CLICK
FOOSH
Don't know how I found bathroom or sink. In that sterile light, I felt vacant--purged.
100120.5
like a fever victim shook like a fever victim shook like a fever victim

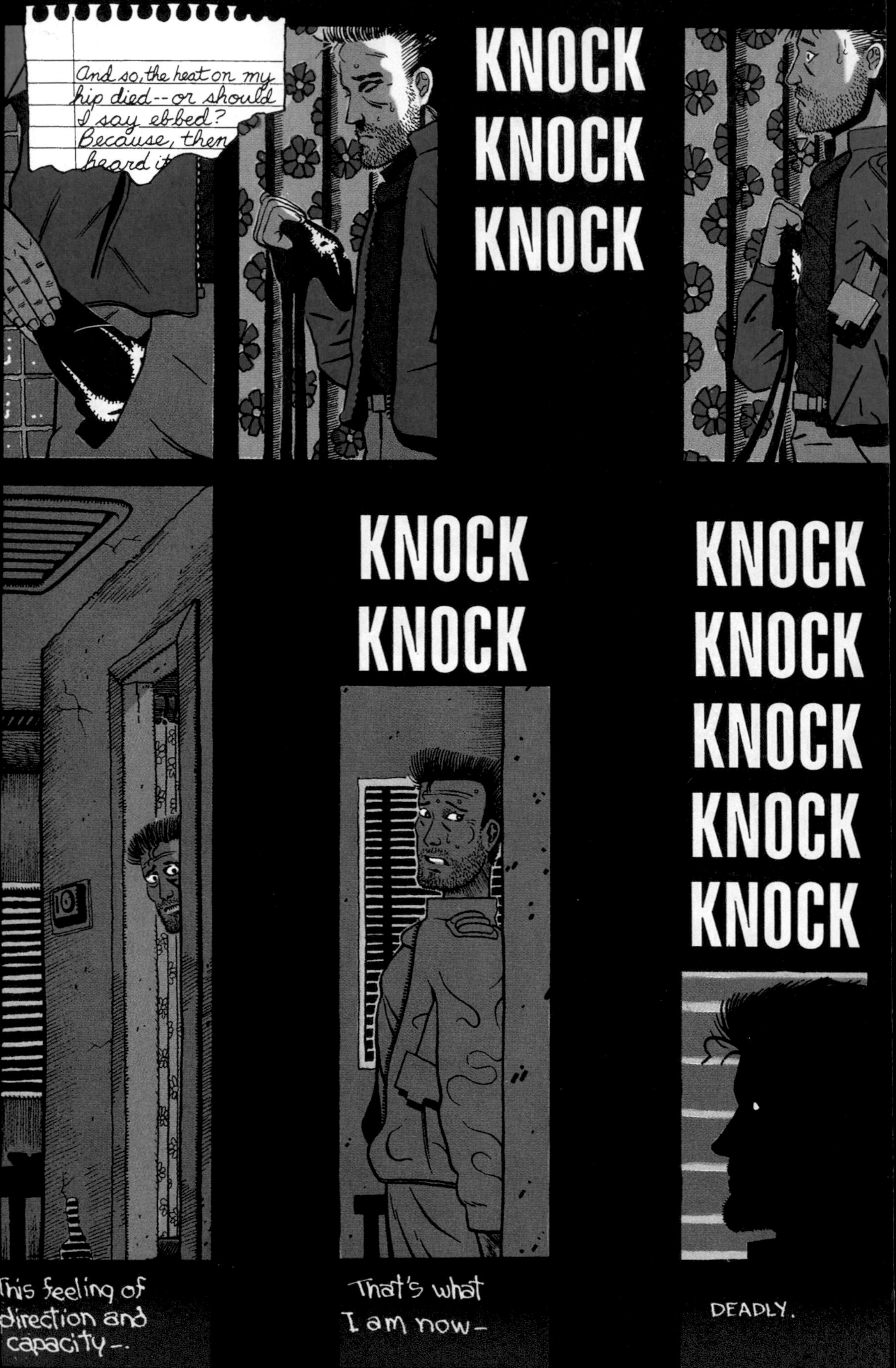
And so, the heat on my hip died--or should I say ebbed? Because, then I heard it
KNOCK
KNOCK
KNOCK
KNOCK
KNOCK
KNOCK
KNOCK
KNOCK
KNOCK
KNOCK
This feeling of direction and capacity--.
That's what I am now-
DEADLY.

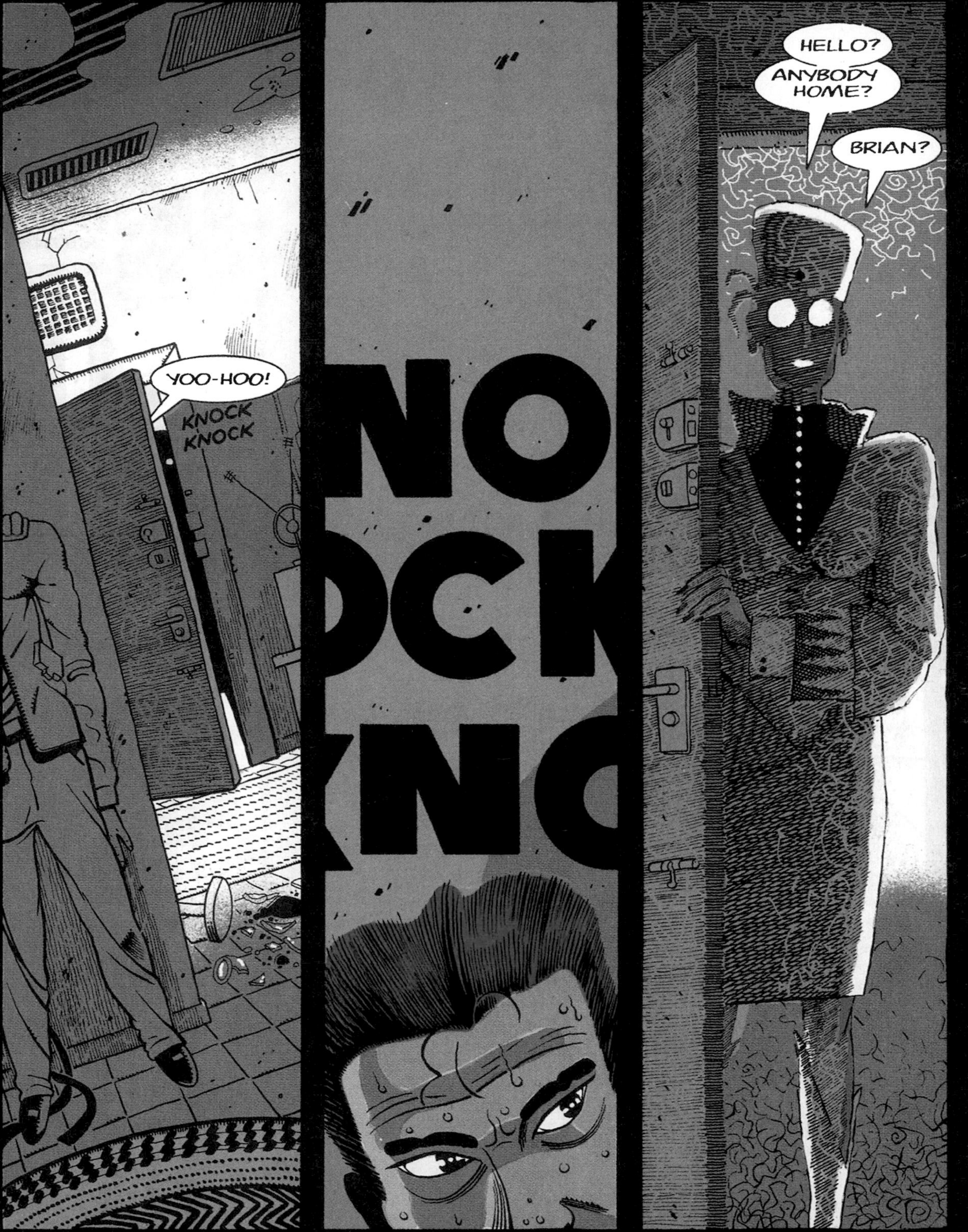
YOO-HOO!
KNOCK KNOCK
NO
OCK
KNO
HELLO?
ANYBODY HOME?
BRIAN?

I was ready.

I'm patient.

I'm directed.

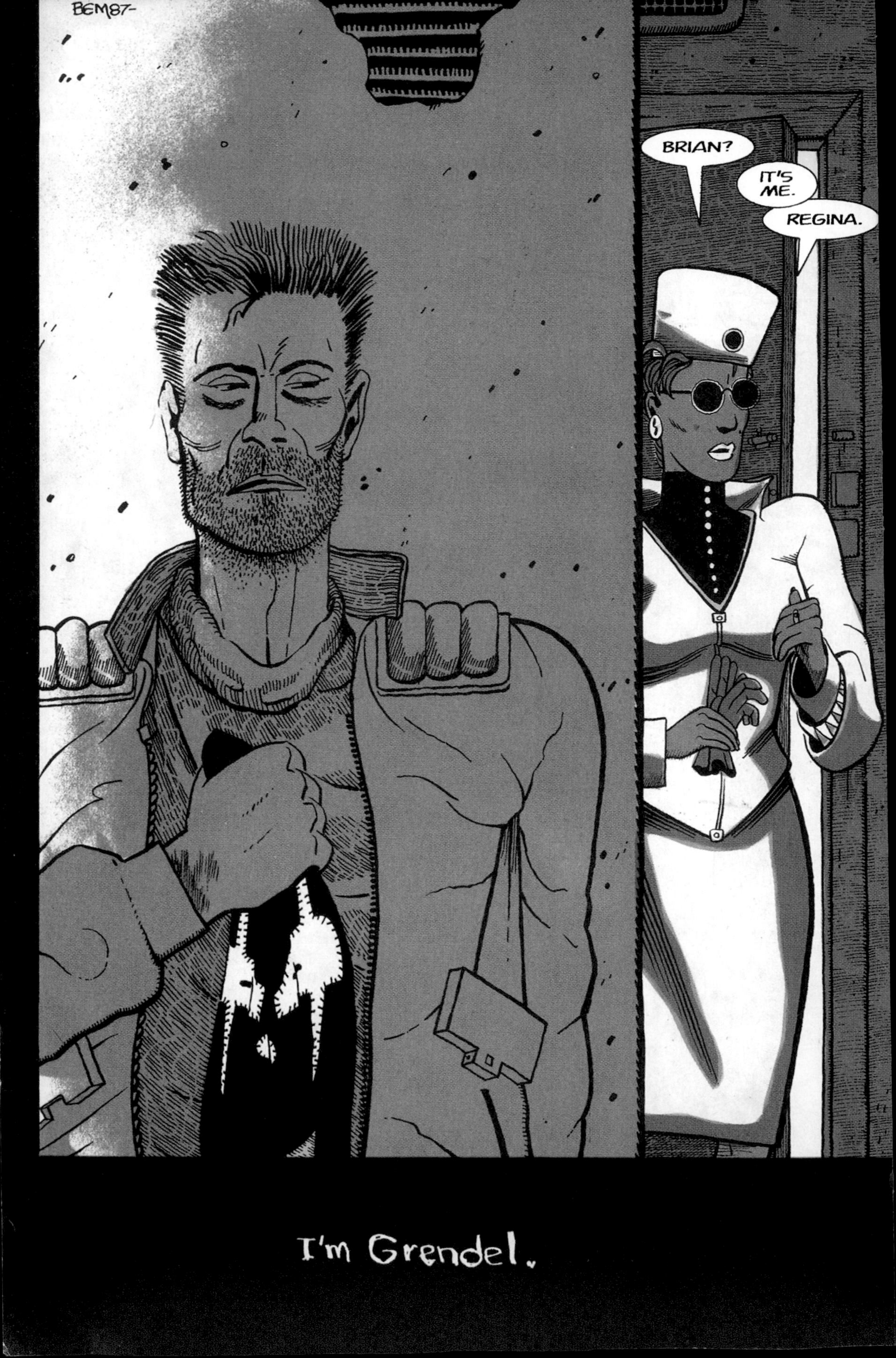
BEM87-
BRIAN?
IT'S ME.
REGINA.

I'm Grendel.

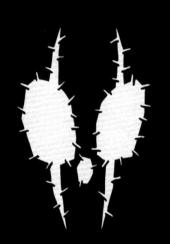

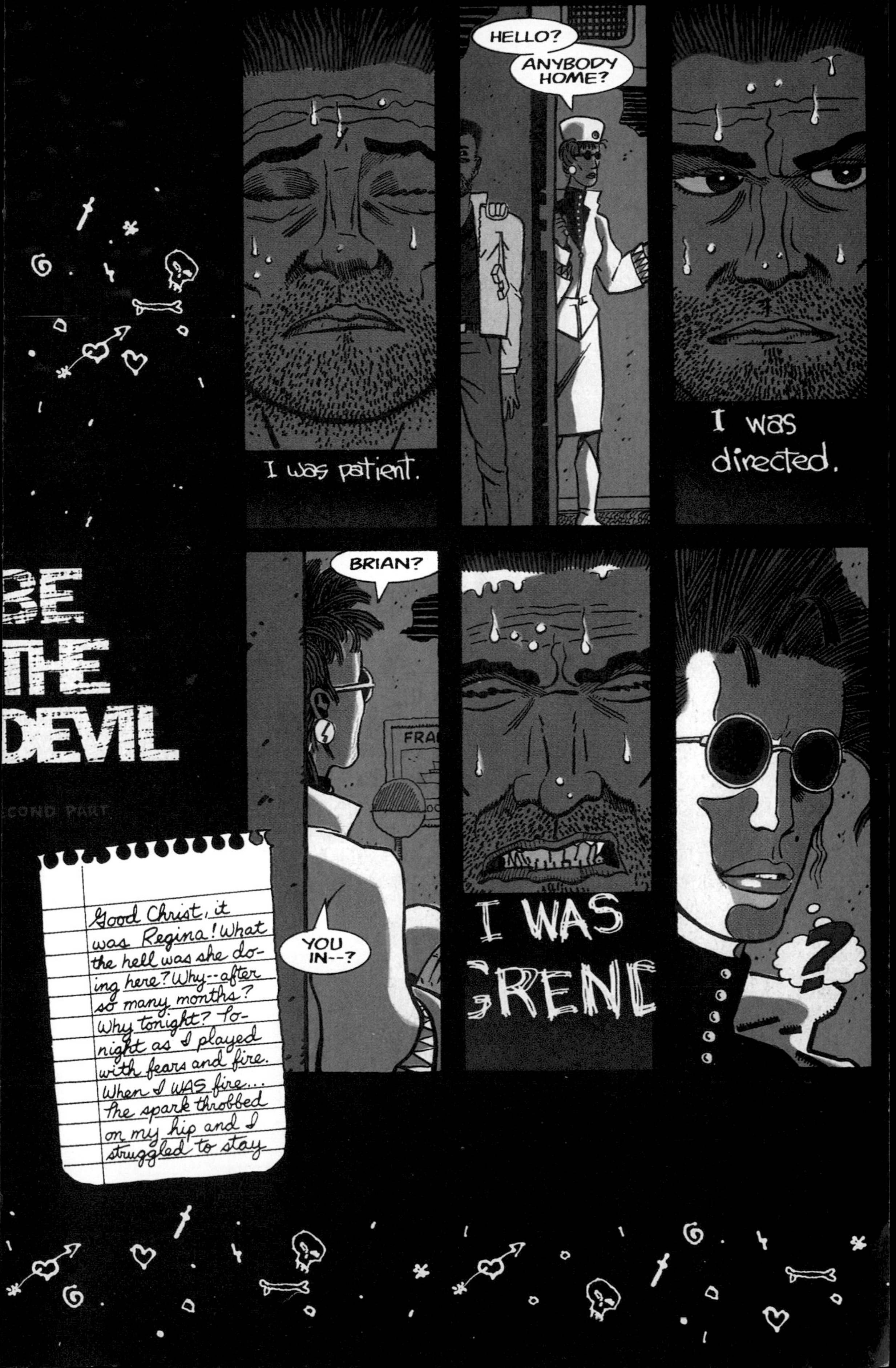
BE THE DEVIL
COND PART
I was patient.
HELLO?
ANYBODY HOME?
I was directed.
BRIAN?
YOU IN--?
I WAS
GREND
Good Christ, it was Regina! What the hell was she doing here? Why--after so many months? Why tonight? Tonight as I played with fears and fire. When I WAS fire... the spark throbbed on my hip and I struggled to stay

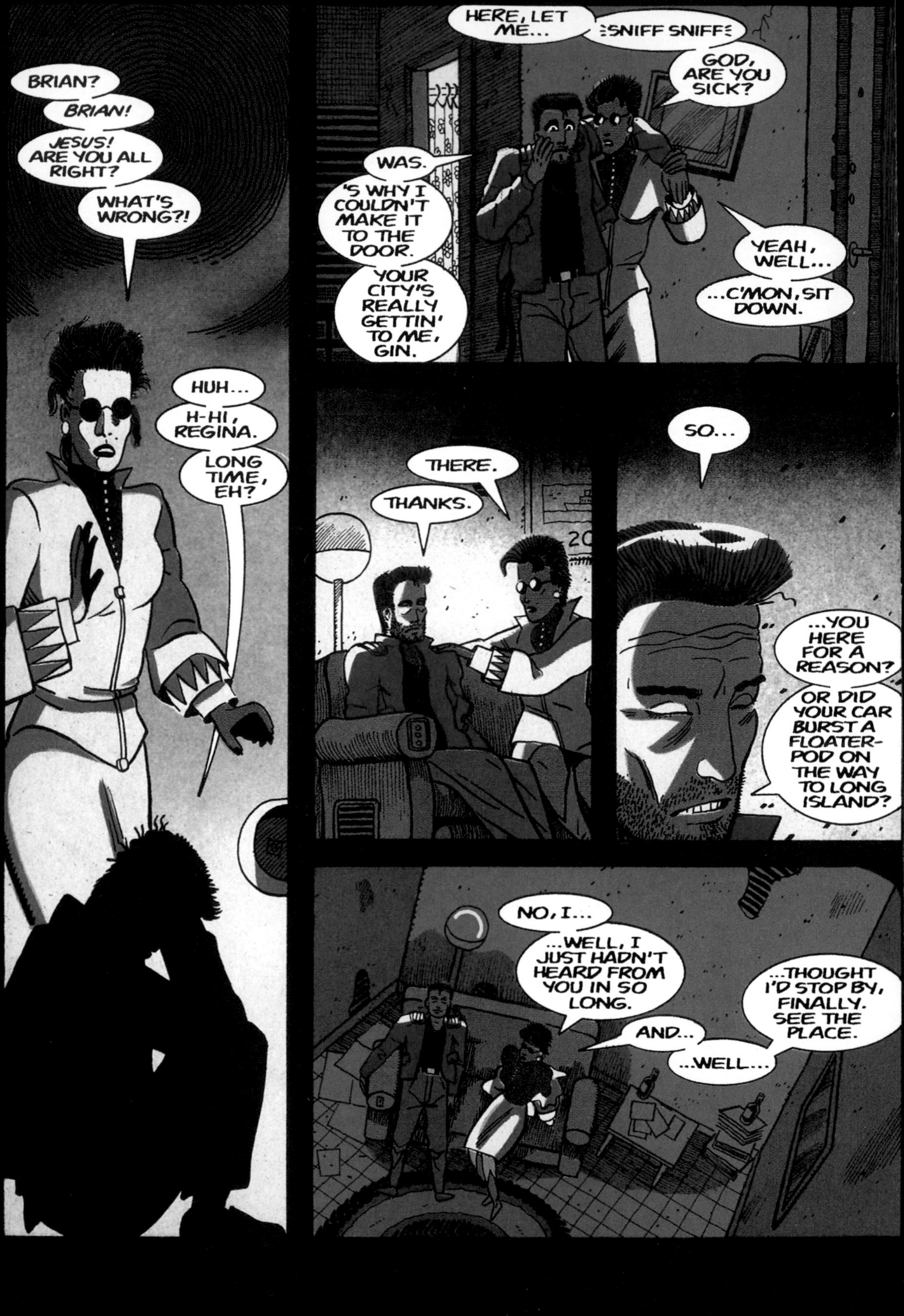
BRIAN?
BRIAN!
JESUS! ARE YOU ALL RIGHT?
WHAT'S WRONG?!
HUH...
H-HI, REGINA.
LONG TIME, EH?
HERE, LET ME...
SNIFF SNIFF
GOD, ARE YOU SICK?
WAS.
'S WHY I COULDN'T MAKE IT TO THE DOOR.
YOUR CITY'S REALLY GETTIN' TO ME, GIN.
YEAH, WELL...
...C'MON, SIT DOWN.
THERE.
THANKS.
SO...
...YOU HERE FOR A REASON?
OR DID YOUR CAR BURST A FLOATER-POD ON THE WAY TO LONG ISLAND?
NO, I...
...WELL, I JUST HADN'T HEARD FROM YOU IN SO LONG.
AND...
...WELL...
...THOUGHT I'D STOP BY, FINALLY. SEE THE PLACE.

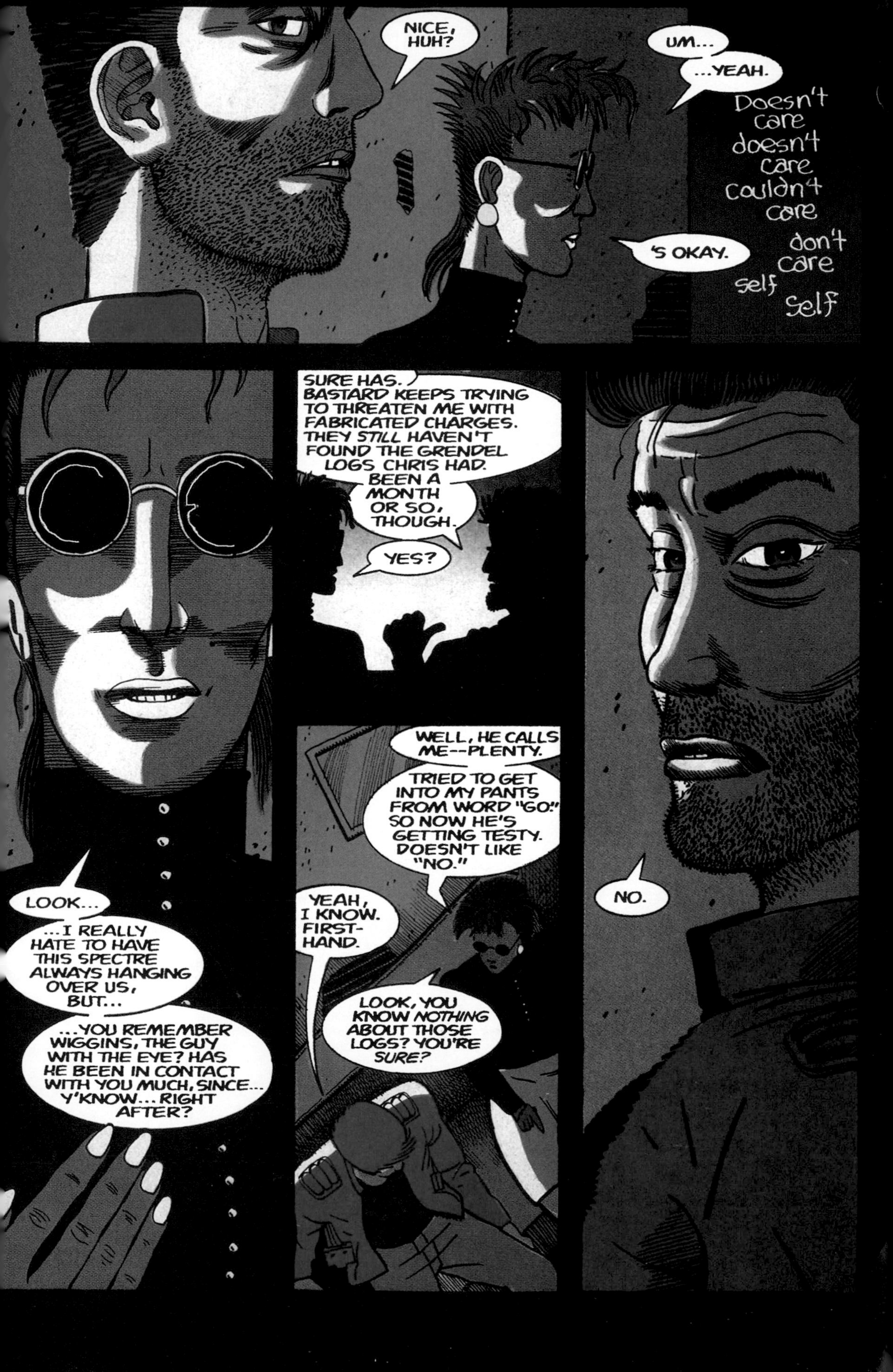
NICE, HUH?
UM...
...YEAH.
Doesn't care doesn't care couldn't care
'S OKAY.
don't care self self
SURE HAS. BASTARD KEEPS TRYING TO THREATEN ME WITH FABRICATED CHARGES. THEY STILL HAVEN'T FOUND THE GRENDEL LOGS CHRIS HAD. BEEN A MONTH OR SO, THOUGH.
YES?
LOOK...
...I REALLY HATE TO HAVE THIS SPECTRE ALWAYS HANGING OVER US, BUT...
...YOU REMEMBER WIGGINS, THE GUY WITH THE EYE? HAS HE BEEN IN CONTACT WITH YOU MUCH, SINCE... Y'KNOW... RIGHT AFTER?
WELL, HE CALLS ME--PLENTY.
TRIED TO GET INTO MY PANTS FROM WORD "GO." SO NOW HE'S GETTING TESTY. DOESN'T LIKE "NO."
YEAH, I KNOW. FIRST-HAND.
LOOK, YOU KNOW NOTHING ABOUT THOSE LOGS? YOU'RE SURE?
NO.

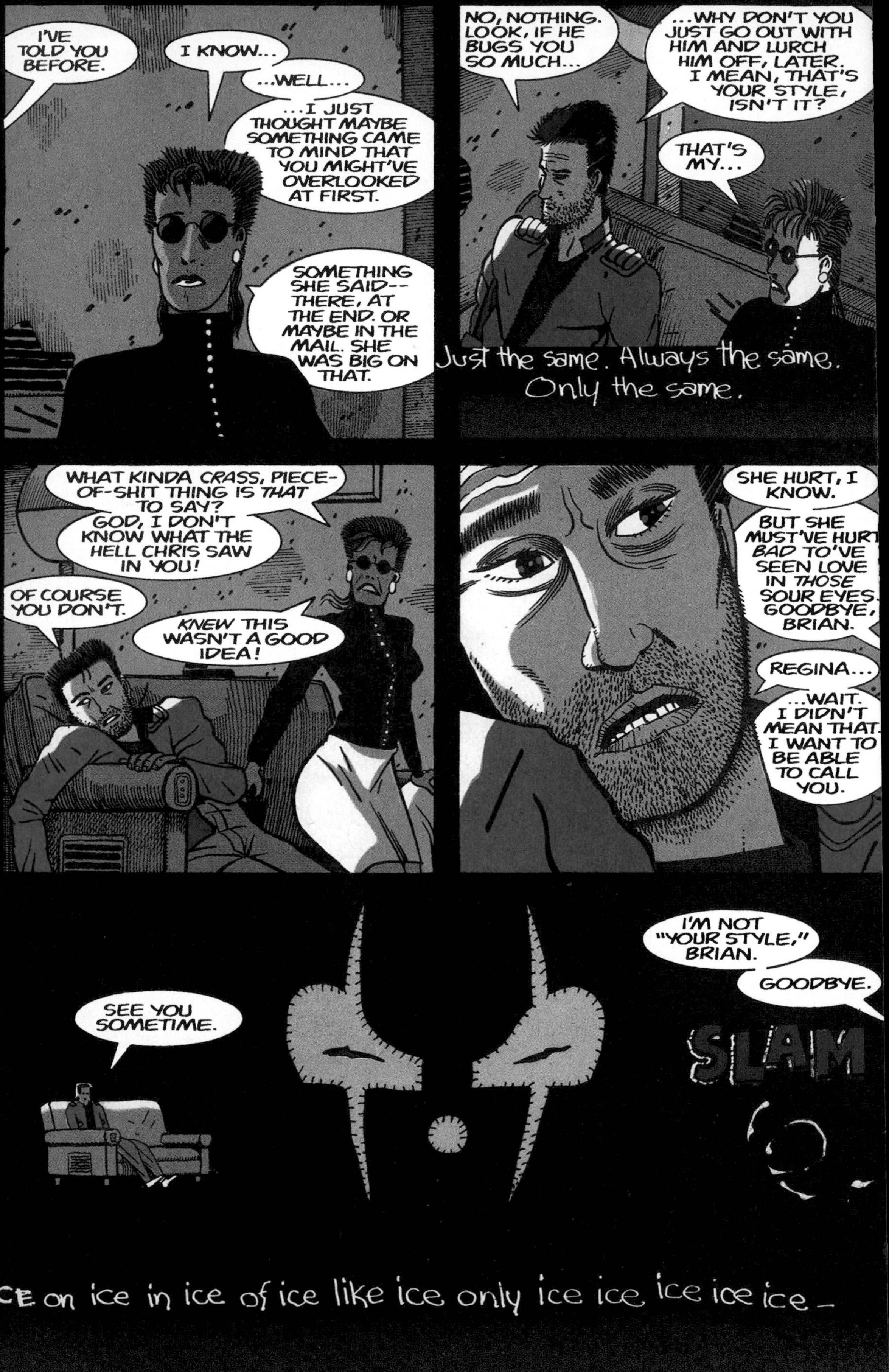

I'VE TOLD YOU BEFORE.
I KNOW...
...WELL...
...I JUST THOUGHT MAYBE SOMETHING CAME TO MIND THAT YOU MIGHT'VE OVERLOOKED AT FIRST.
SOMETHING SHE SAID-- THERE, AT THE END. OR MAYBE IN THE MAIL. SHE WAS BIG ON THAT.
NO, NOTHING. LOOK, IF HE BUGS YOU SO MUCH...
...WHY DON'T YOU JUST GO OUT WITH HIM AND LURCH HIM OFF, LATER. I MEAN, THAT'S YOUR STYLE, ISN'T IT?
THAT'S MY...
Just the same. Always the same. Only the same.
WHAT KINDA CRASS, PIECE-OF-SHIT THING IS THAT TO SAY? GOD, I DON'T KNOW WHAT THE HELL CHRIS SAW IN YOU!
OF COURSE YOU DON'T.
KNEW THIS WASN'T A GOOD IDEA!
SHE HURT, I KNOW.
BUT SHE MUST'VE HURT BAD TO'VE SEEN LOVE IN THOSE SOUR EYES. GOODBYE, BRIAN.
REGINA...
...WAIT. I DIDN'T MEAN THAT. I WANT TO BE ABLE TO CALL YOU.
I'M NOT "YOUR STYLE," BRIAN.
GOODBYE.
SEE YOU SOMETIME.
SLAM
ICE on ice in ice of ice like ice only ice ice ice ice ice –

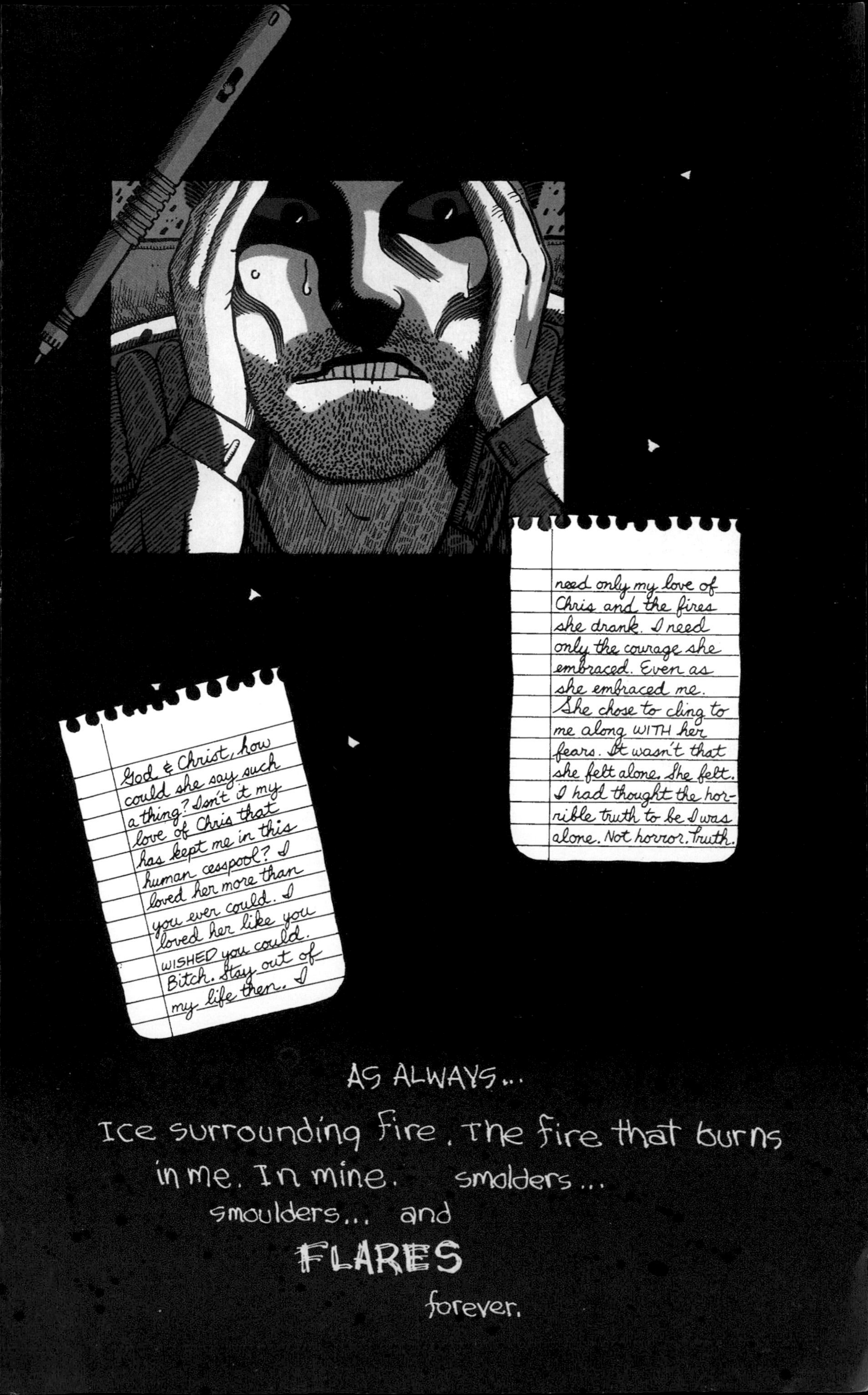
God & Christ, how could she say such a thing? Isn't it my love of Chris that has kept me in this human cesspool? I loved her more than you ever could. I loved her like you WISHED you could. Bitch. Stay out of my life then. I
need only my love of Chris and the fires she drank. I need only the courage she embraced. Even as she embraced me. She chose to cling to me along WITH her fears. It wasn't that she felt alone. She felt. I had thought the horrible truth to be I was alone. Not horror. Truth.
AS ALWAYS...
Ice surrounding fire. The fire that burns in me. In mine. smolders...
smoulders... and
FLARES
forever.

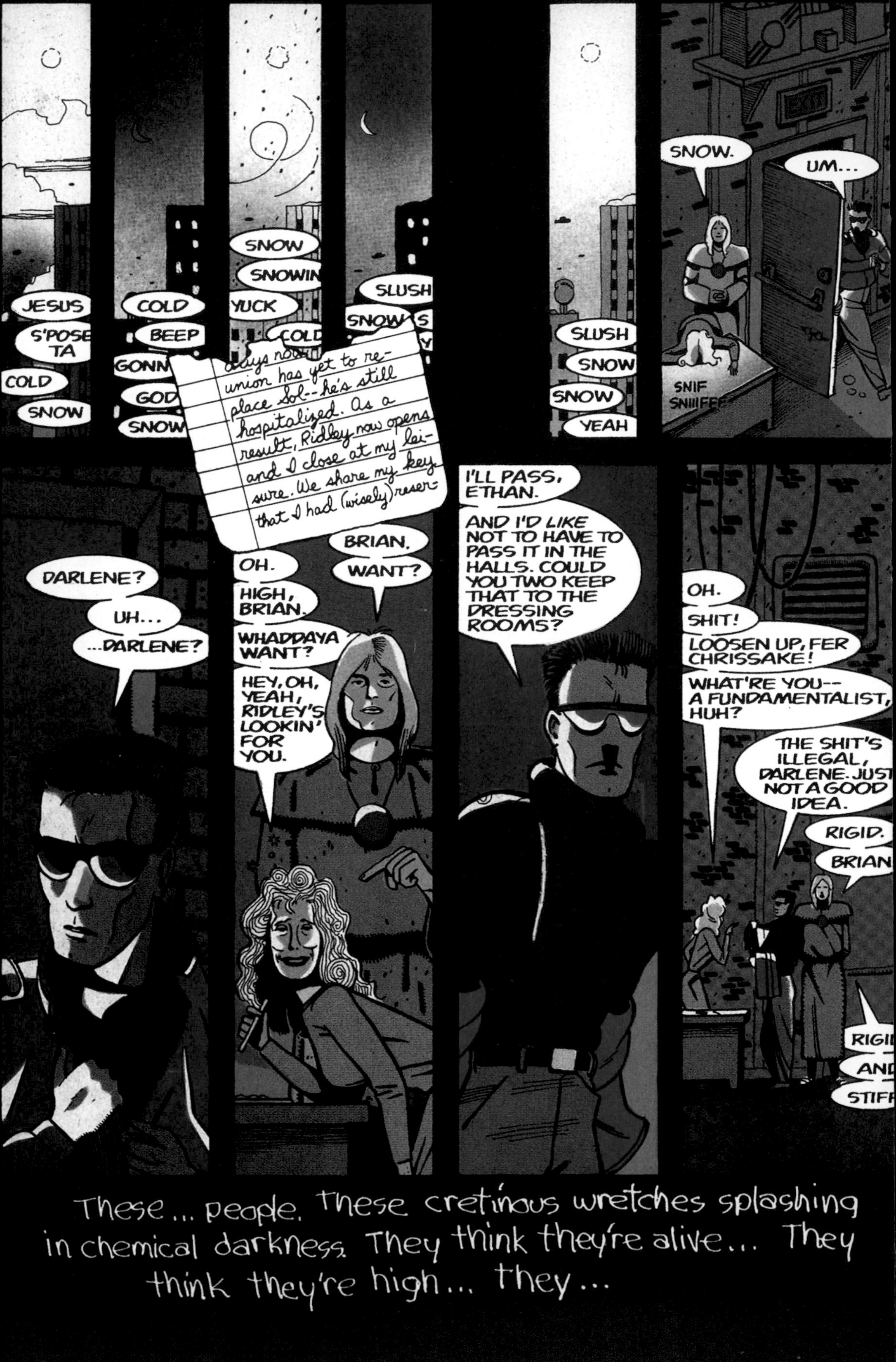
JESUS
S'POSE TA
COLD
SNOW
COLD
BEEP
GONN
GOD
SNOW
SNOW
SNOWIN
YUCK
COLD
SLUSH
SNOW
days now ... union has yet to re- place Sol--he's still hospitalized. As a result, Ridley now opens and I close at my lei- sure. We share my key that I had (wisely) reser-
SLUSH
SNOW
SNOW
YEAH
SNOW.
UM...
SNIF
SNIIIFFF
DARLENE?
UH...
...DARLENE?
OH.
HIGH, BRIAN.
WHADDAYA WANT?
HEY, OH, YEAH, RIDLEY'S LOOKIN' FOR YOU.
BRIAN.
WANT?
I'LL PASS, ETHAN.
AND I'D LIKE NOT TO HAVE TO PASS IT IN THE HALLS. COULD YOU TWO KEEP THAT TO THE DRESSING ROOMS?
OH.
SHIT!
LOOSEN UP, FER CHRISSAKE!
WHAT'RE YOU-- A FUNDAMENTALIST, HUH?
THE SHIT'S ILLEGAL, DARLENE. JUST NOT A GOOD IDEA.
RIGID.
BRIAN
RIGI
AND
STIFF

These... people. These cretinous wretches splashing in chemical darkness. They think they're alive... They think they're high... they...

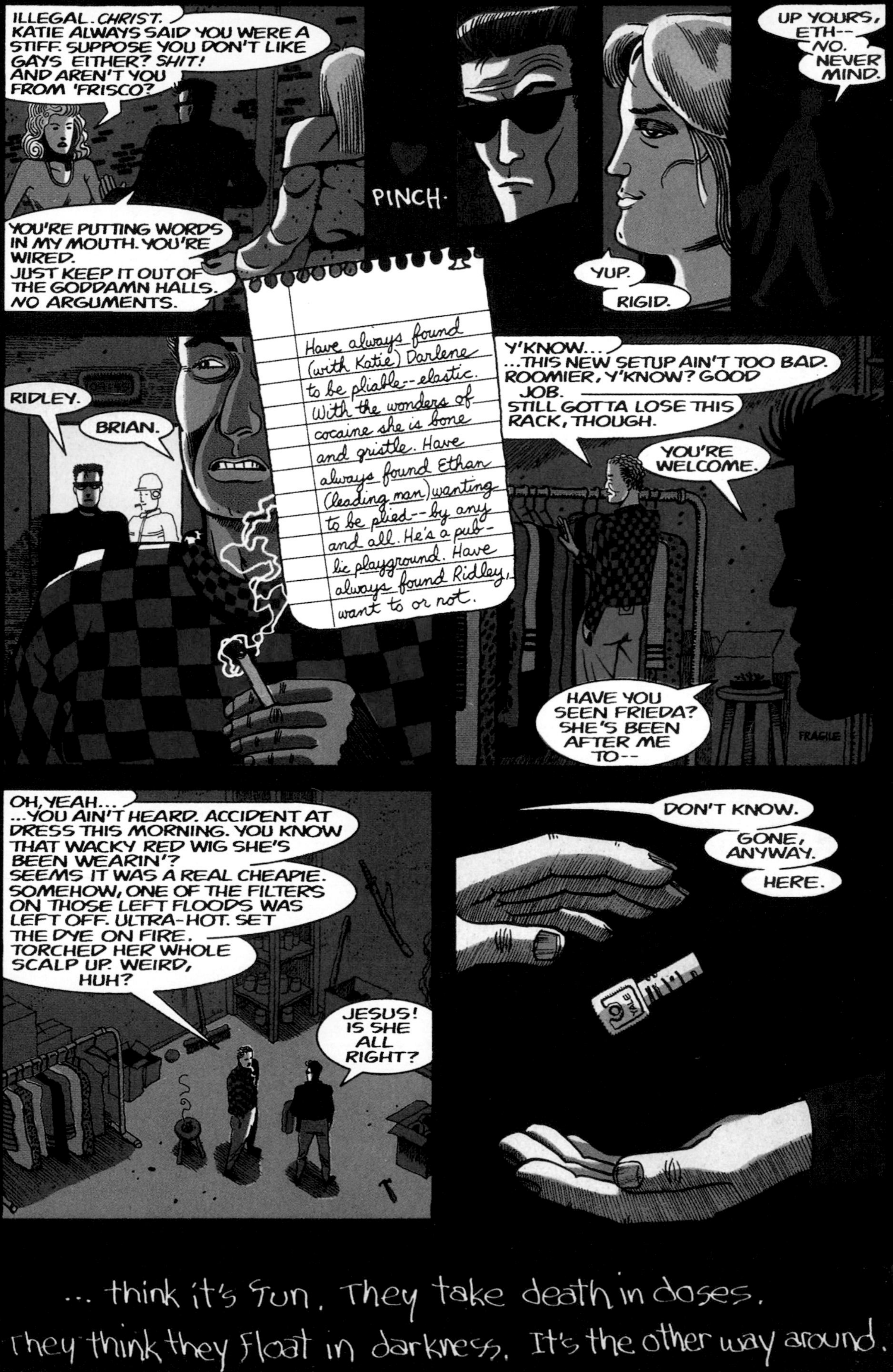
ILLEGAL. CHRIST. KATIE ALWAYS SAID YOU WERE A STIFF. SUPPOSE YOU DON'T LIKE GAYS EITHER? SHIT! AND AREN'T YOU FROM 'FRISCO?
YOU'RE PUTTING WORDS IN MY MOUTH. YOU'RE WIRED. JUST KEEP IT OUT OF THE GODDAMN HALLS. NO ARGUMENTS.
PINCH.
UP YOURS, ETH-- NO. NEVER MIND.
YUP.
RIGID.
Have always found (with Katie) Darlene to be pliable--elastic. With the wonders of cocaine she is bone and gristle. Have always found Ethan (leading man) wanting to be plied--by any and all. He's a public playground. Have always found Ridley, want to or not.
RIDLEY.
BRIAN.
Y'KNOW... ...THIS NEW SETUP AIN'T TOO BAD. ROOMIER, Y'KNOW? GOOD JOB. STILL GOTTA LOSE THIS RACK, THOUGH.
YOU'RE WELCOME.
HAVE YOU SEEN FRIEDA? SHE'S BEEN AFTER ME TO--
FRAGILE
OH, YEAH... ...YOU AIN'T HEARD. ACCIDENT AT DRESS THIS MORNING. YOU KNOW THAT WACKY RED WIG SHE'S BEEN WEARIN'? SEEMS IT WAS A REAL CHEAPIE. SOMEHOW, ONE OF THE FILTERS ON THOSE LEFT FLOODS WAS LEFT OFF. ULTRA-HOT. SET THE DYE ON FIRE. TORCHED HER WHOLE SCALP UP. WEIRD, HUH?
JESUS! IS SHE ALL RIGHT?
DON'T KNOW.
GONE, ANYWAY.
HERE.
YALE
... think it's fun. They take death in doses.
They think they float in darkness. It's the other way around.

ANYHOW...
...DARLENE WAS HER UNDERSTUDY, SO NOW SHE'S LEAD. LITTLE PUSS HAS HER HEAD IN THE CLOUDS.

REALLY.

YEAH.

SO, NO MORE FRIEDA TO DEAL WITH, HEY?

I KNOW WHAT A PAIN IN YOUR ASS SHE WAS.

My little CHICKADEE...

WELL... ...GOTTA SEE ABOUT A NEW SOFA FOR SCENE TWO OLD ONE'S FOR SHIT. DO SOMETHIN' 'BOUT THAT RACK.

YEAH

YEAH. SURE.

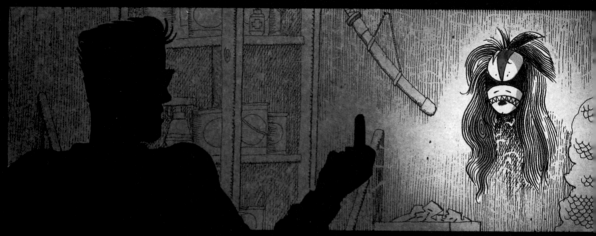

Heh Heh Heh Heh -- yes, they float... they eddy, while

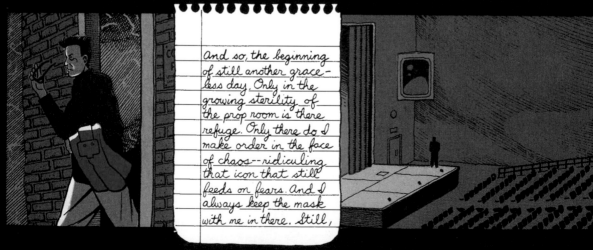

And so, the beginning of still another grace-less day. Only in the growing sterility of the prop room is there refuge. Only there do I make order in the face of chaos--ridiculing that icon that still feeds on fears. And I always keep the mask with me in there. Still,

I can only swim with strokes swift and sure.

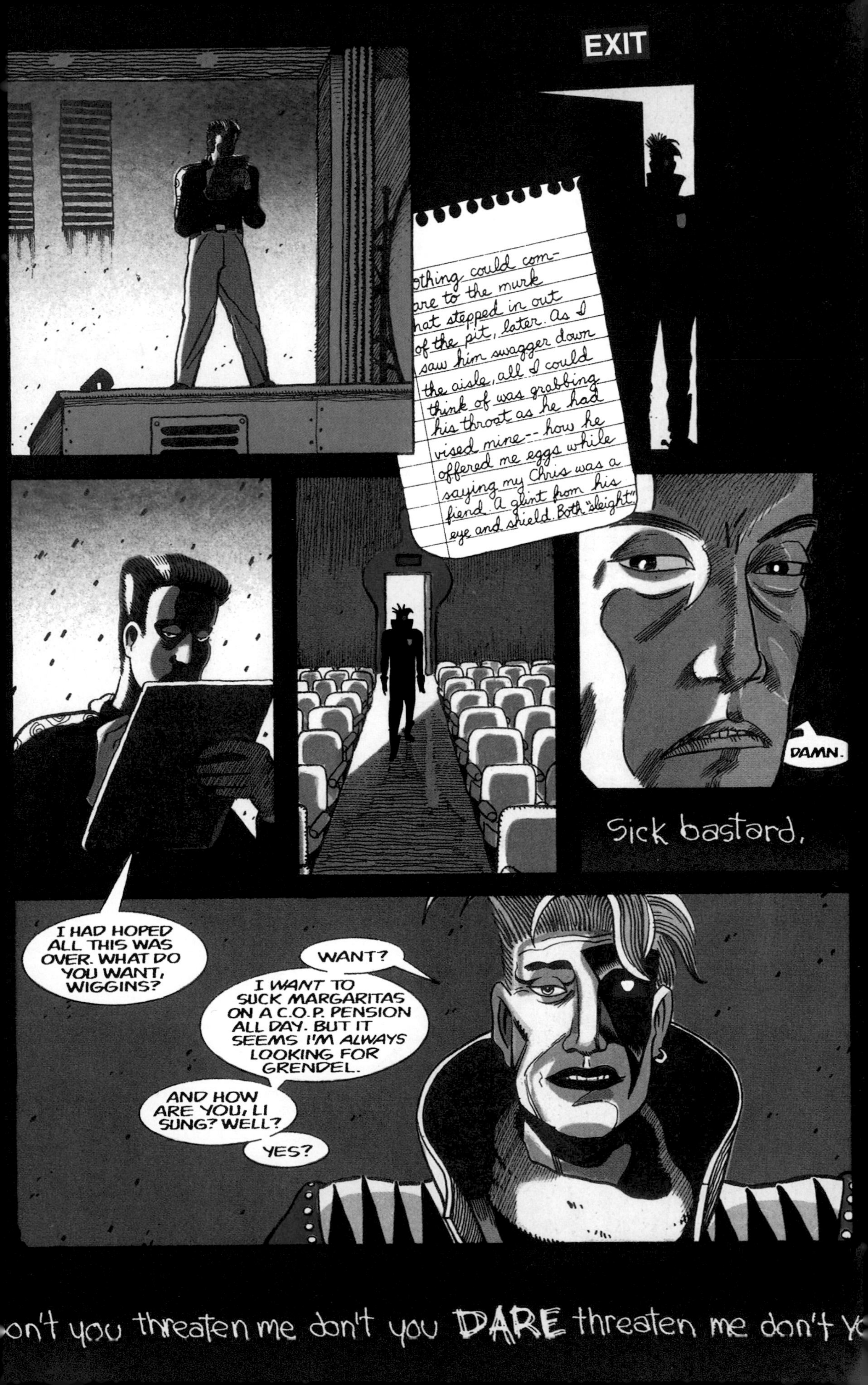
EXIT
othing could com-
are to the murk
hat stepped in out
of the pit, later. As I
saw him swagger down
the aisle, all I could
think of was grabbing
his throat as he had
vised mine-- how he
offered me eggs while
saying my Chris was a
fiend. A glint from his
eye and shield. Both "sleight."
DAMN.
Sick bastard.
I HAD HOPED ALL THIS WAS OVER. WHAT DO YOU WANT, WIGGINS?
WANT?
I WANT TO SUCK MARGARITAS ON A C.O.P. PENSION ALL DAY. BUT IT SEEMS I'M ALWAYS LOOKING FOR GRENDEL.
AND HOW ARE YOU, LI SUNG? WELL?
YES?
on't you threaten me don't you DARE threaten me don't yo

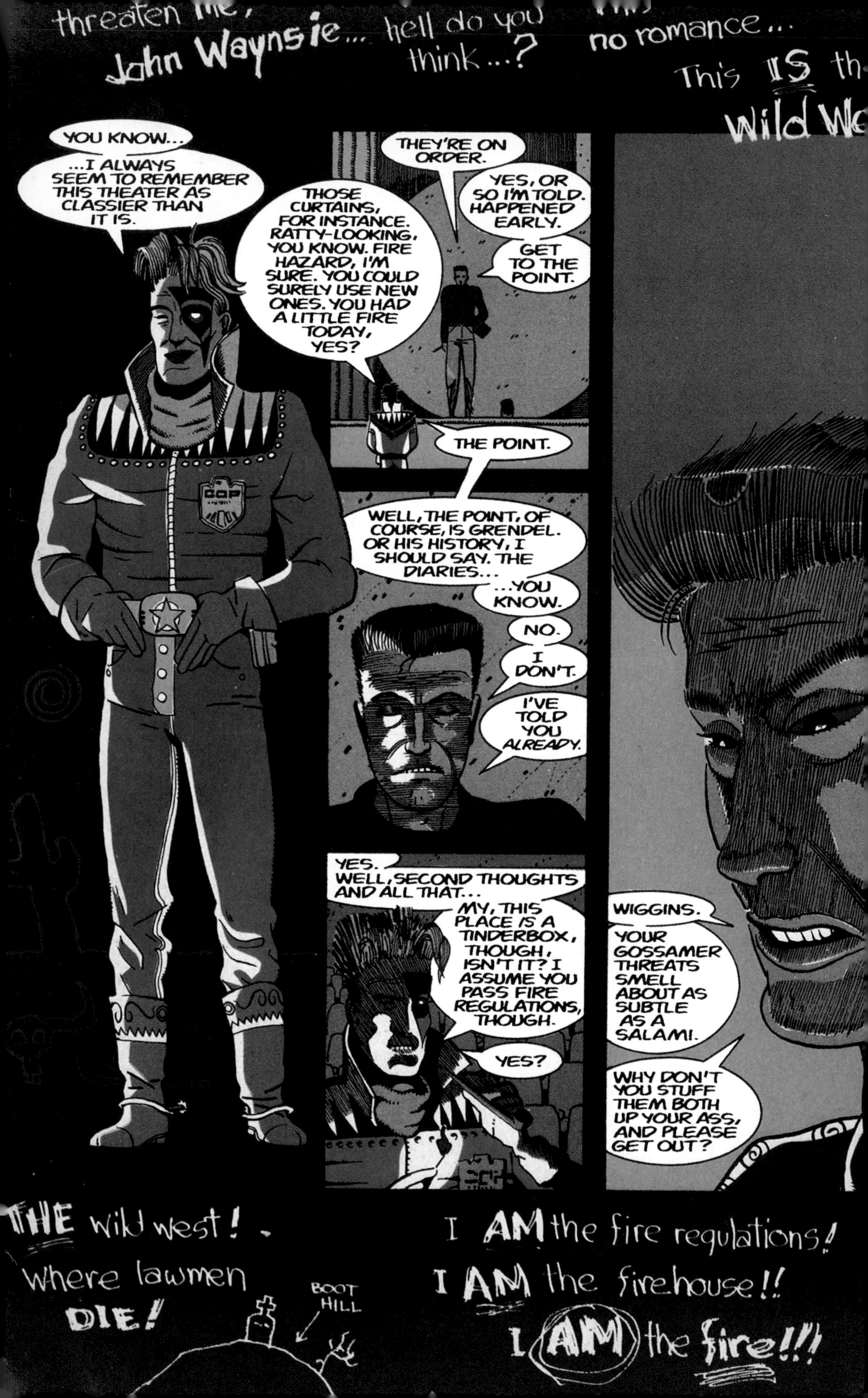

threaten me,
John Waynsie... hell do you think...?
no romance...
This IS the Wild We
YOU KNOW...
...I ALWAYS SEEM TO REMEMBER THIS THEATER AS CLASSIER THAN IT IS.
THOSE CURTAINS, FOR INSTANCE. RATTY-LOOKING, YOU KNOW. FIRE HAZARD, I'M SURE. YOU COULD SURELY USE NEW ONES. YOU HAD A LITTLE FIRE TODAY, YES?
THEY'RE ON ORDER.
YES, OR SO I'M TOLD. HAPPENED EARLY.
GET TO THE POINT.
THE POINT.
WELL, THE POINT, OF COURSE, IS GRENDEL. OR HIS HISTORY, I SHOULD SAY. THE DIARIES...
...YOU KNOW.
NO.
I DON'T.
I'VE TOLD YOU ALREADY.
YES. WELL, SECOND THOUGHTS AND ALL THAT...
MY, THIS PLACE IS A TINDERBOX, THOUGH, ISN'T IT? I ASSUME YOU PASS FIRE REGULATIONS, THOUGH.
YES?
WIGGINS.
YOUR GOSSAMER THREATS SMELL ABOUT AS SUBTLE AS A SALAMI.
WHY DON'T YOU STUFF THEM BOTH UP YOUR ASS, AND PLEASE GET OUT?
THE wild west! Where lawmen DIE!
BOOT HILL
I AM the fire regulations!
I AM the firehouse!!
I AM the fire!!!

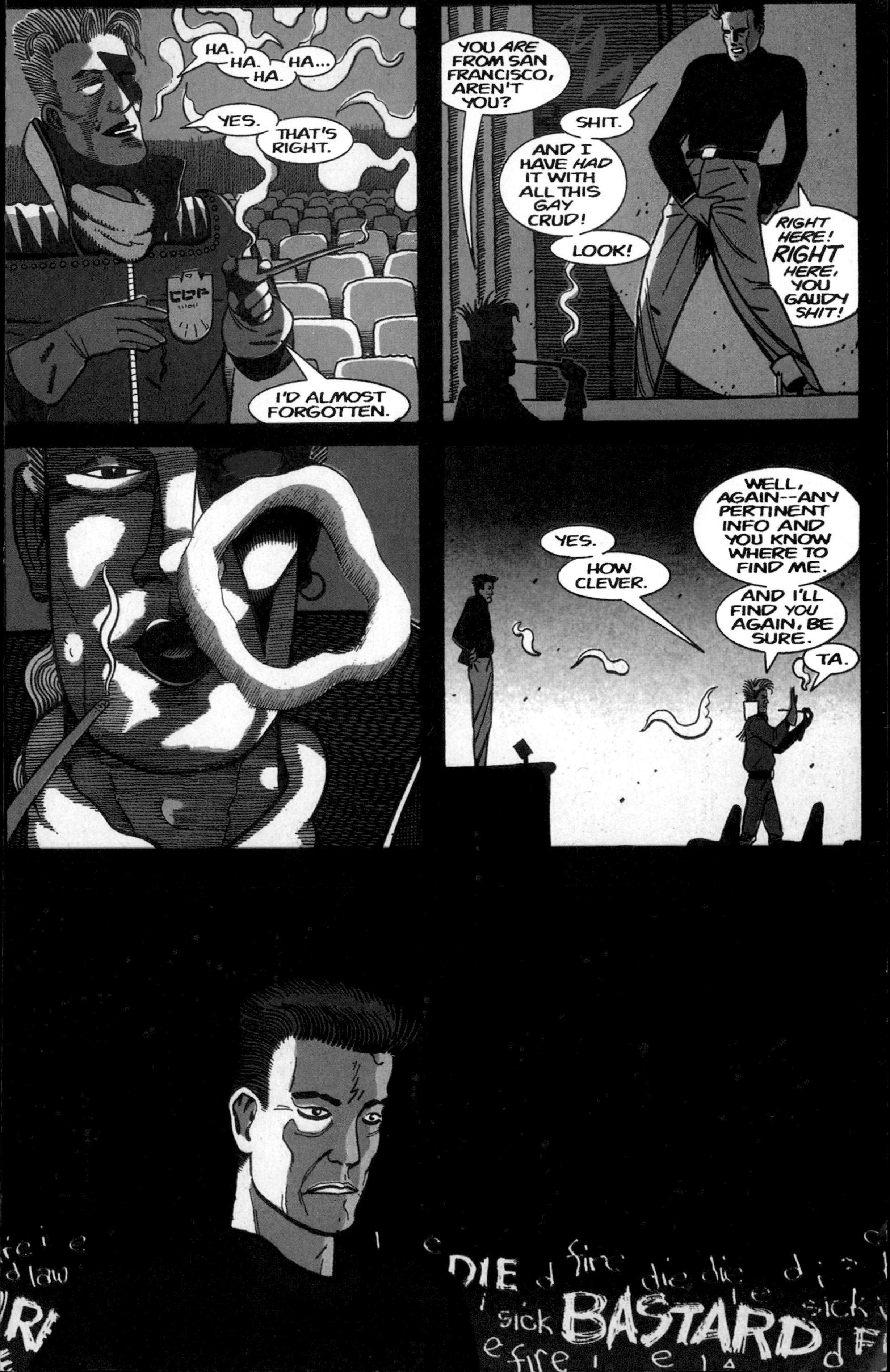
HA. HA. HA. HA...
YES. THAT'S RIGHT.
I'D ALMOST FORGOTTEN.
YOU *ARE* FROM SAN FRANCISCO, AREN'T YOU?
SHIT.
AND I HAVE *HAD* IT WITH ALL THIS GAY CRUD!
LOOK!
RIGHT HERE! **RIGHT** *HERE, YOU GAUDY SHIT!*
YES.
HOW CLEVER.
WELL, AGAIN--ANY PERTINENT INFO AND YOU KNOW WHERE TO FIND ME.
AND I'LL FIND YOU AGAIN, BE SURE.
TA.
law
DIE
fire
die die
sick
BASTARD
fire

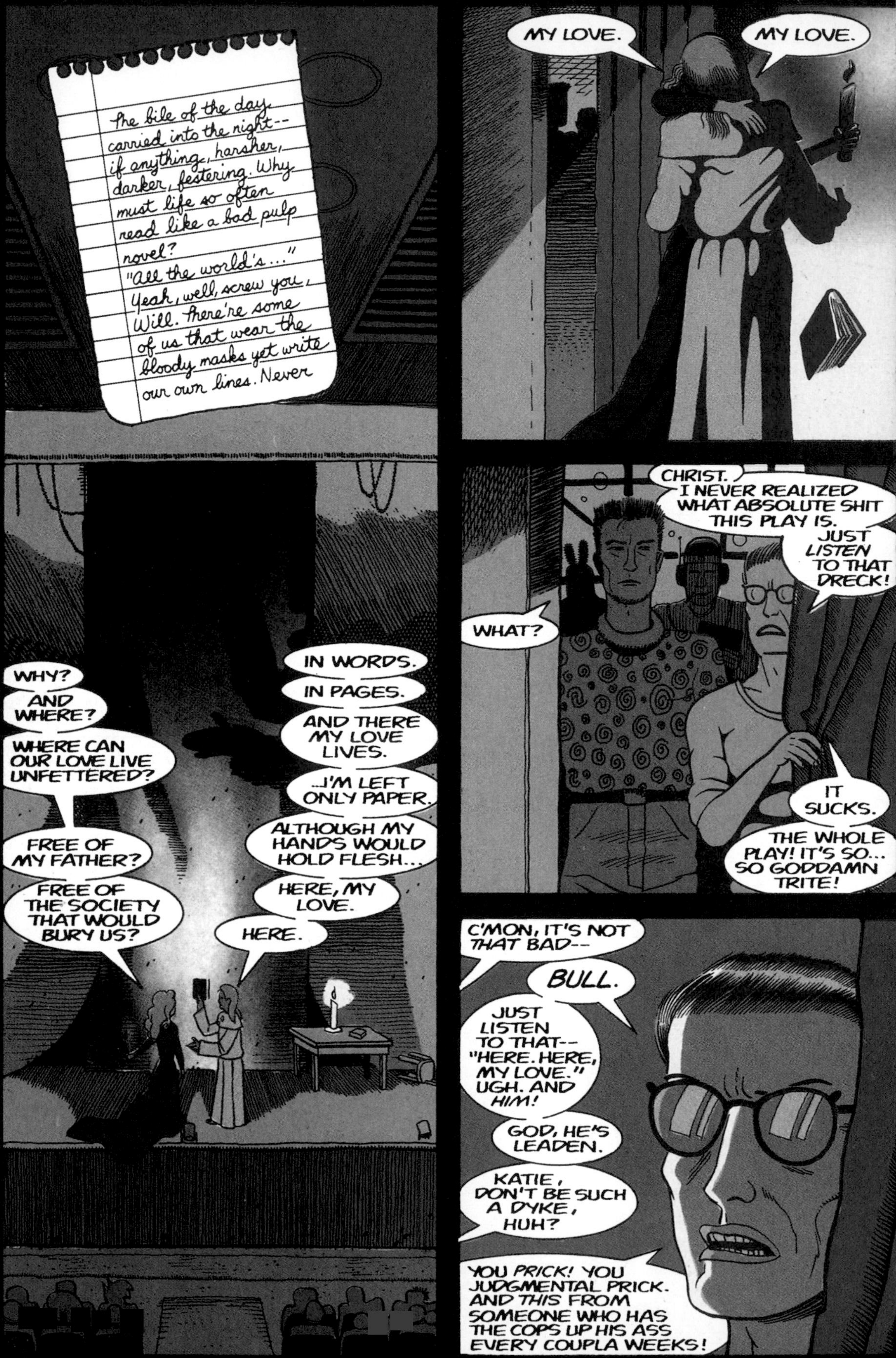
The bile of the day carried into the night-- if anything, harsher, darker, festering. Why must life so often read like a bad pulp novel?
"All the world's..."
Yeah, well, screw you, Will. There're some of us that wear the bloody masks yet write our own lines. Never
MY LOVE.
MY LOVE.
WHY?
AND WHERE?
WHERE CAN OUR LOVE LIVE UNFETTERED?
FREE OF MY FATHER?
FREE OF THE SOCIETY THAT WOULD BURY US?
IN WORDS.
IN PAGES.
AND THERE MY LOVE LIVES.
...I'M LEFT ONLY PAPER.
ALTHOUGH MY HANDS WOULD HOLD FLESH...
HERE, MY LOVE.
HERE.
CHRIST. I NEVER REALIZED WHAT ABSOLUTE SHIT THIS PLAY IS.
JUST LISTEN TO THAT DRECK!
WHAT?
IT SUCKS.
THE WHOLE PLAY! IT'S SO... SO GODDAMN TRITE!
C'MON, IT'S NOT THAT BAD--
BULL.
JUST LISTEN TO THAT-- "HERE. HERE, MY LOVE." UGH. AND HIM!
GOD, HE'S LEADEN.
KATIE, DON'T BE SUCH A DYKE, HUH?
YOU PRICK! YOU JUDGMENTAL PRICK. AND THIS FROM SOMEONE WHO HAS THE COPS UP HIS ASS EVERY COUPLA WEEKS!

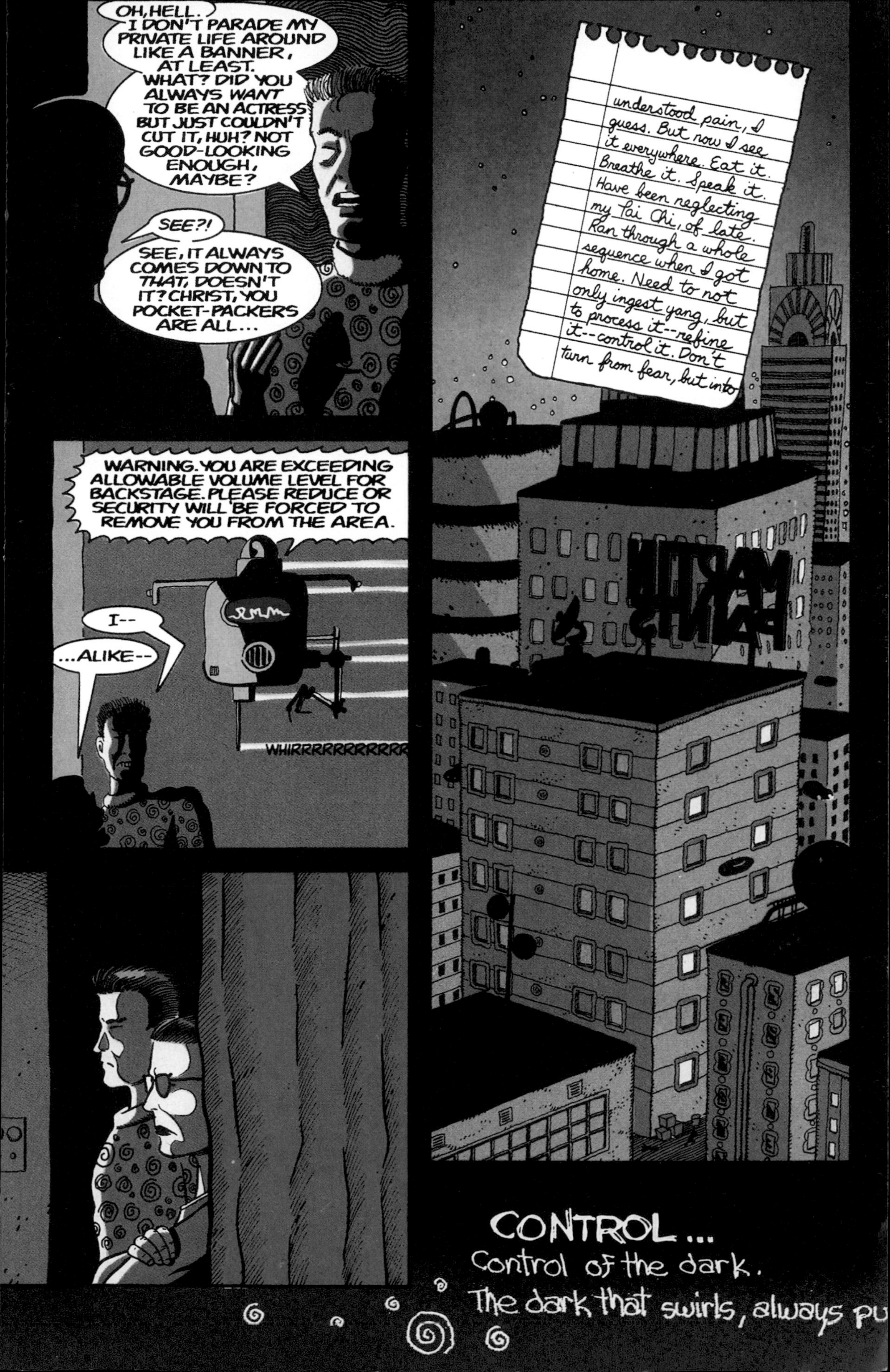
OH, HELL. I DON'T PARADE MY PRIVATE LIFE AROUND LIKE A BANNER, AT LEAST.
WHAT? DID YOU ALWAYS WANT TO BE AN ACTRESS BUT JUST COULDN'T CUT IT, HUH? NOT GOOD-LOOKING ENOUGH, MAYBE?
SEE?!
SEE, IT ALWAYS COMES DOWN TO THAT, DOESN'T IT? CHRIST, YOU POCKET-PACKERS ARE ALL...
understood pain, I guess. But now I see it everywhere. Eat it. Breathe it. Speak it. Have been neglecting my Tai Chi, of late. Ran through a whole sequence when I got home. Need to not only ingest yang, but to process it--refine it--control it. Don't turn from fear, but into
WARNING. YOU ARE EXCEEDING ALLOWABLE VOLUME LEVEL FOR BACKSTAGE. PLEASE REDUCE OR SECURITY WILL BE FORCED TO REMOVE YOU FROM THE AREA.
I--
...ALIKE--
WHIRRRRRRRRRRR
CONTROL...
Control of the dark.
The dark that swirls, always pu

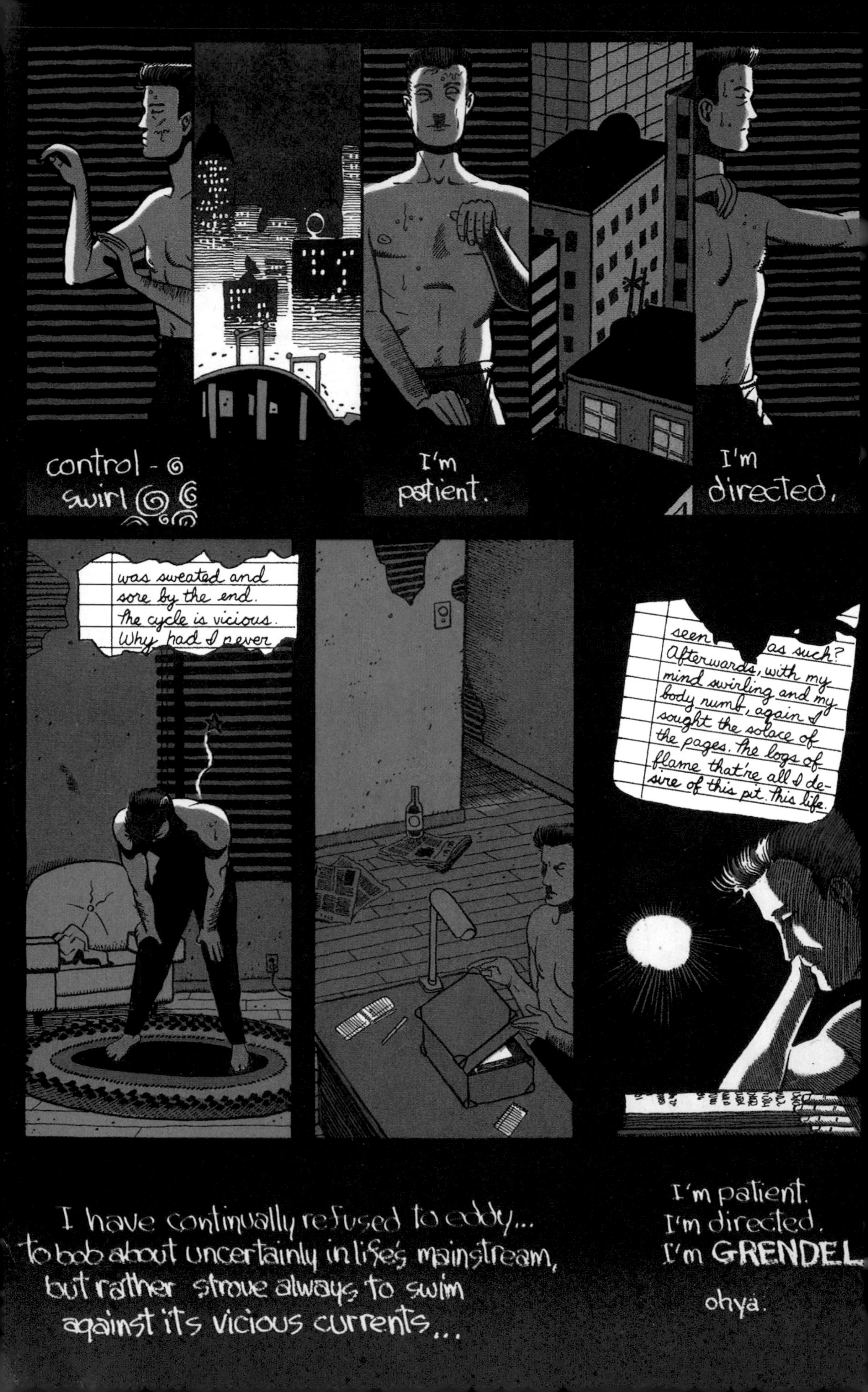
control - swirl
I'm patient.
I'm directed.
was sweated and sore by the end. The cycle is vicious. Why had I never
seen as such? Afterwards, with my mind swirling and my body numb, again I sought the solace of the pages. The logs of flame that're all I desire of this pit. This life.
I have continually refused to eddy... to bob about uncertainly in life's mainstream, but rather strove always to swim against its vicious currents...
I'm patient.
I'm directed.
I'm GRENDEL.
ohya.

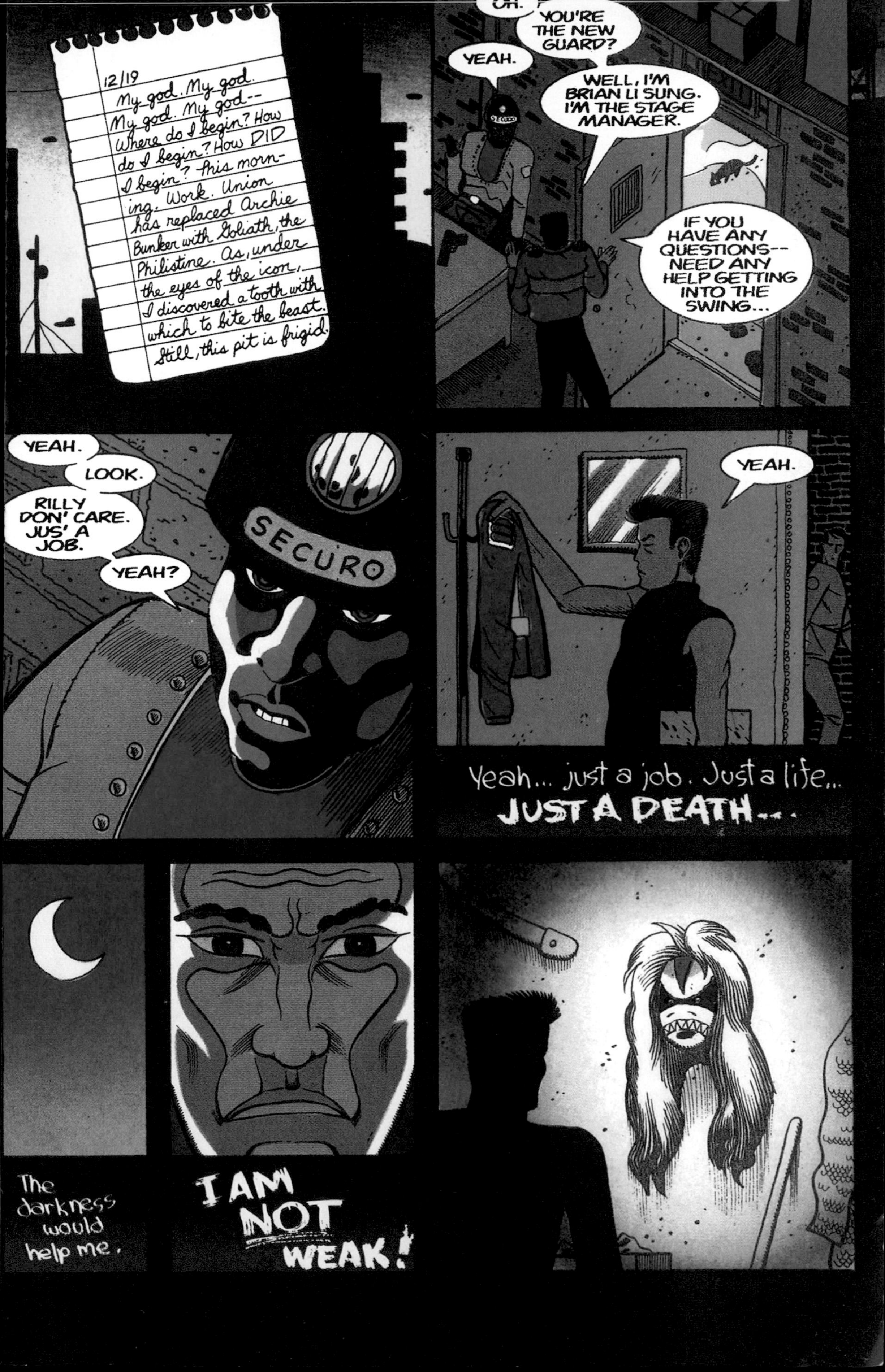
12/19
My god. My god. My god. My god-- Where do I begin? How do I begin? How DID I begin? This morning. Work. Union has replaced Archie Bunker with Goliath, the Philistine. As, under the eyes of the icon, I discovered a tooth with which to bite the beast. Still, this pit is frigid.
YOU'RE THE NEW GUARD?
YEAH.
WELL, I'M BRIAN LI SUNG. I'M THE STAGE MANAGER.
IF YOU HAVE ANY QUESTIONS-- NEED ANY HELP GETTING INTO THE SWING...
YEAH.
LOOK.
RILLY DON' CARE. JUS' A JOB.
YEAH?
SECURO
YEAH.
Yeah... just a job. Just a life... JUST A DEATH...
The darkness would help me.
I AM NOT WEAK!

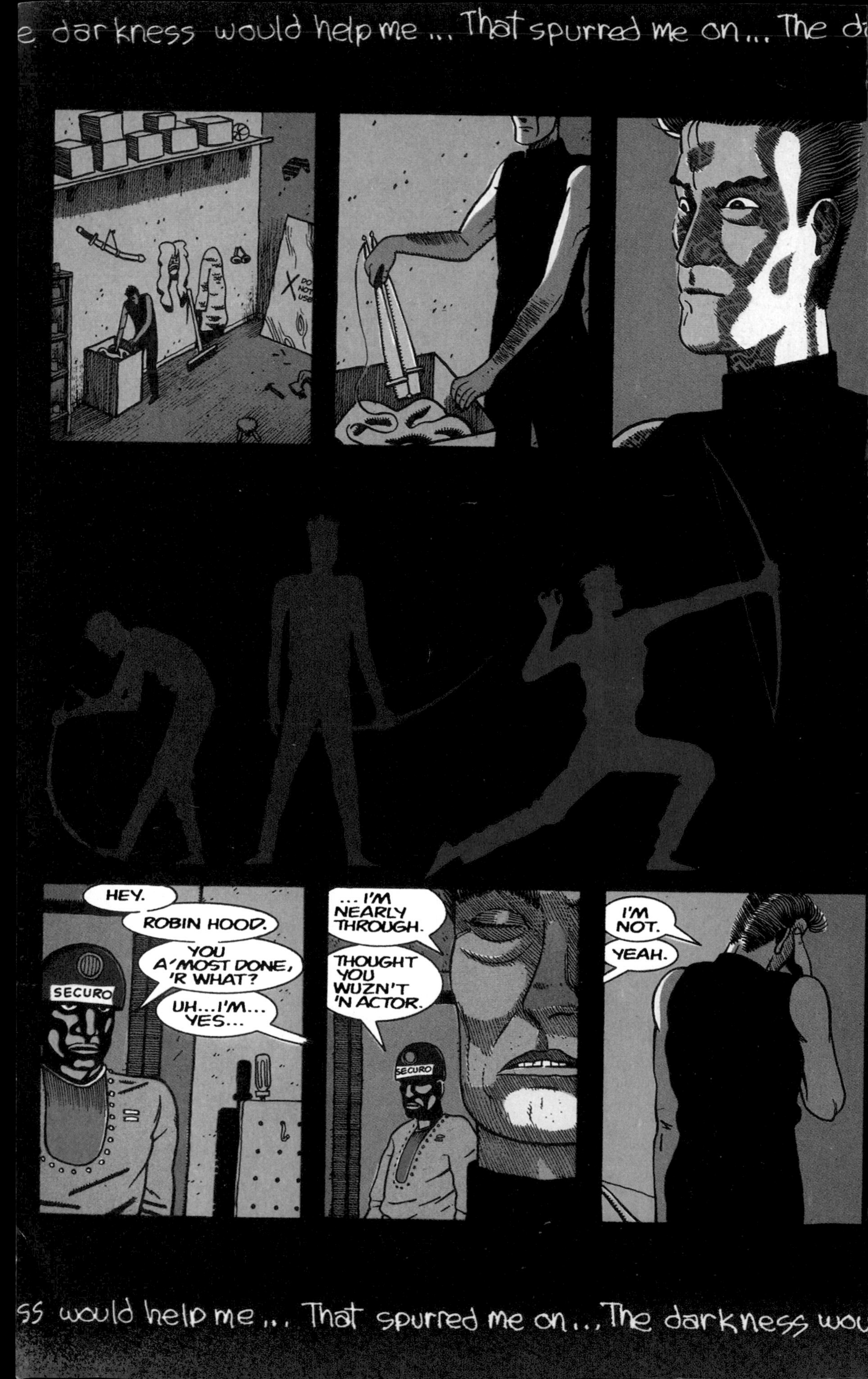
e darkness would help me... That spurred me on... The da
HEY.
ROBIN HOOD.
YOU A'MOST DONE, 'R WHAT?
UH... I'M... YES...
... I'M NEARLY THROUGH.
THOUGHT YOU WUZN'T 'N ACTOR.
I'M NOT.
YEAH.
ss would help me... That spurred me on... The darkness wou

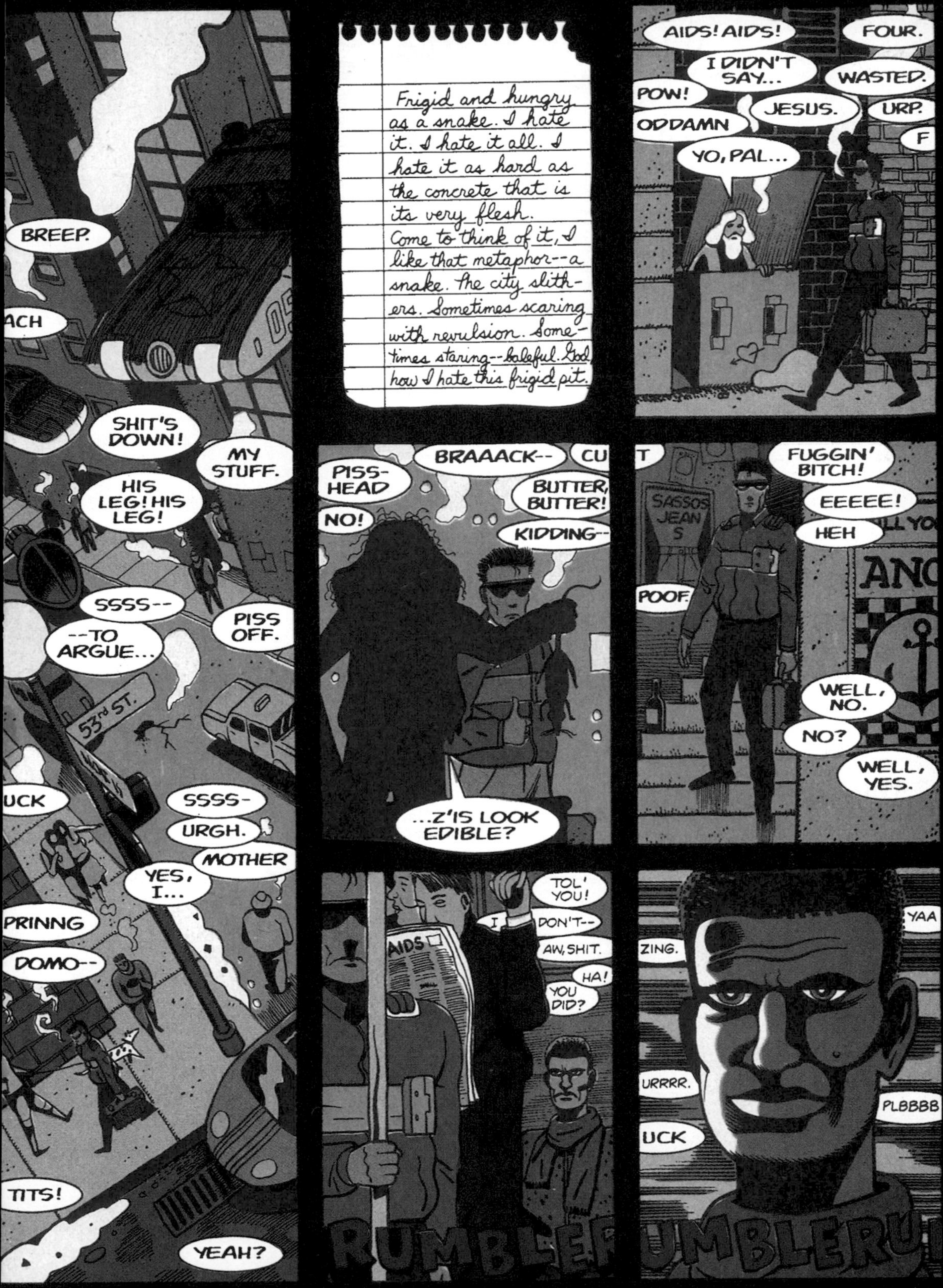
BREEP.
ACH
SHIT'S DOWN!
MY STUFF.
HIS LEG! HIS LEG!
SSSS--
PISS OFF.
--TO ARGUE...
53rd ST.
UCK
SSSS-
URGH.
MOTHER
YES, I...
PRINNG
DOMO--
TITS!
YEAH?
Frigid and hungry as a snake. I hate it. I hate it all. I hate it as hard as the concrete that is its very flesh. Come to think of it, I like that metaphor--a snake. The city slithers. Sometimes scaring with revulsion. Sometimes staring--baleful. God how I hate this frigid pit.
AIDS! AIDS!
FOUR.
I DIDN'T SAY...
WASTED.
POW!
JESUS.
URP.
ODDAMN
F
YO, PAL...
PISS-HEAD
BRAAACK--
CU T
BUTTER, BUTTER!
NO!
KIDDING--
...Z'IS LOOK EDIBLE?
FUGGIN' BITCH!
EEEEE!
HEH
SASSOS JEANS
POOF.
WELL, NO.
NO?
WELL, YES.
TOL' YOU!
I
DON'T--
AIDS
AW, SHIT.
HA!
YOU DID?
RUMBLER
YAA
ZING.
URRRR.
PLBBBB
UCK
UMBLERU

For it's only **I** who can swim in
the dark-- only **I** that can control the
dark... **AM** the dark.

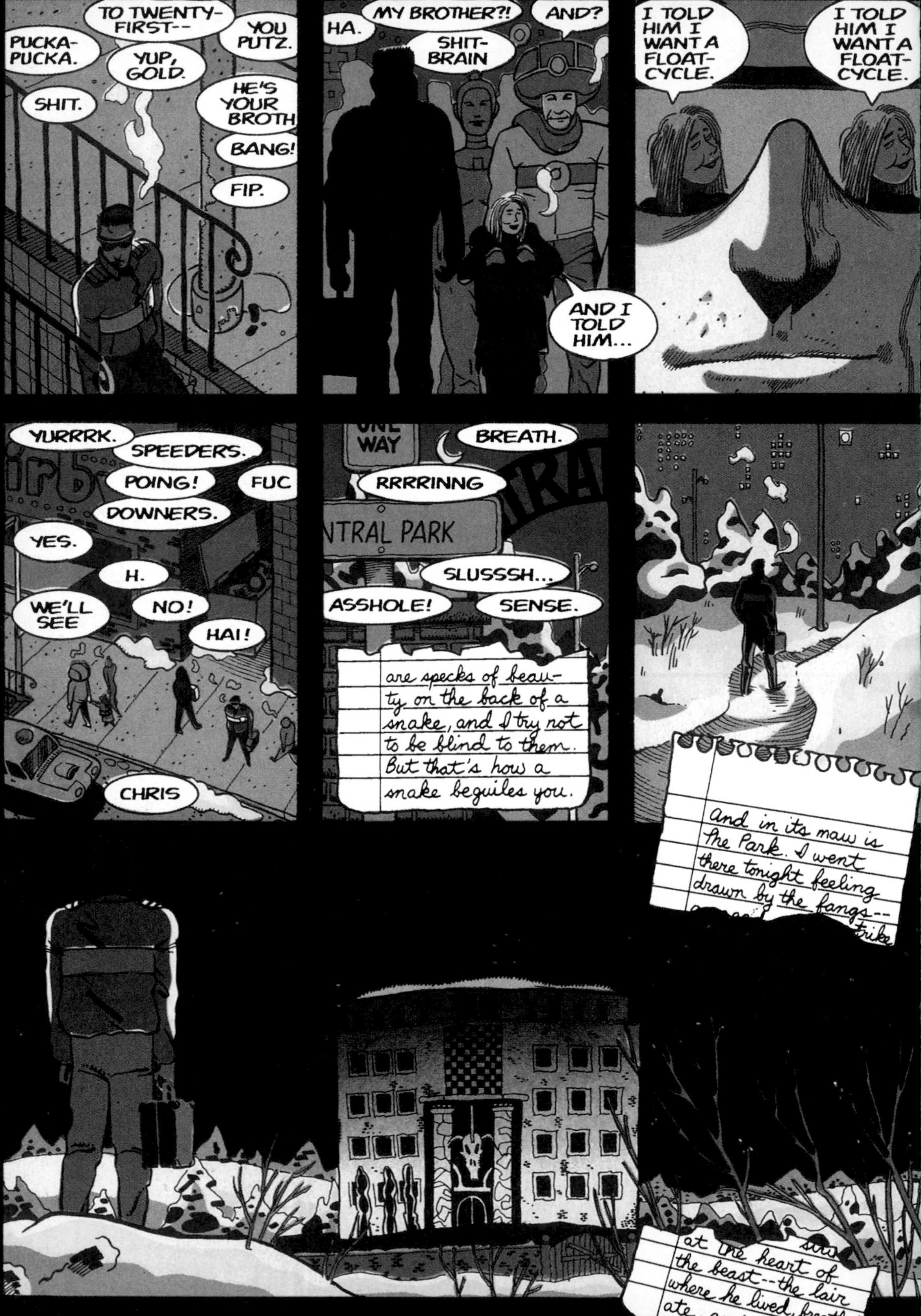
TO TWENTY-FIRST--
PUCKA-PUCKA.
YOU PUTZ.
YUP, GOLD.
SHIT.
HE'S YOUR BROTH
BANG!
FIP.
HA.
MY BROTHER?!
AND?
SHIT-BRAIN
AND I TOLD HIM...
I TOLD HIM I WANT A FLOAT-CYCLE.
I TOLD HIM I WANT A FLOAT-CYCLE.
YURRRK.
SPEEDERS.
POING!
FUC
DOWNERS.
YES.
H.
WE'LL SEE
NO!
HAI!
CHRIS
WAY
BREATH.
RRRRINNG
NTRAL PARK
SLUSSSH...
ASSHOLE!
SENSE.
are specks of beauty on the back of a snake, and I try not to be blind to them. But that's how a snake beguiles you.
And in its maw is The Park. I went there tonight feeling drawn by the fangs--
at the heart of the beast--the lair where he lived, breathed, ate, and shat.

...and I will strike this carnal world...

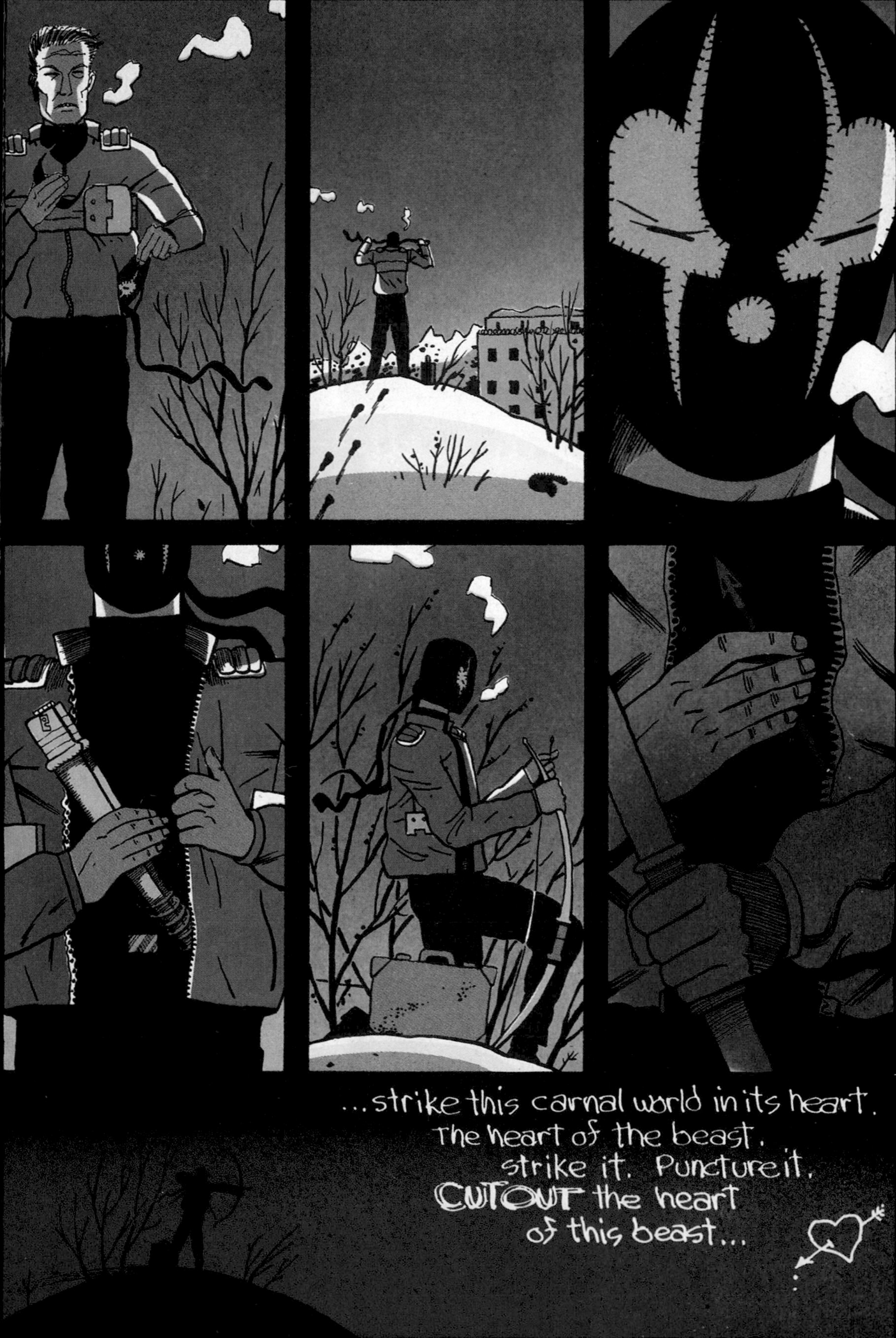
...strike this carnal world in its heart.
The heart of the beast.
strike it. Puncture it.
CUTOUT the heart
of this beast...

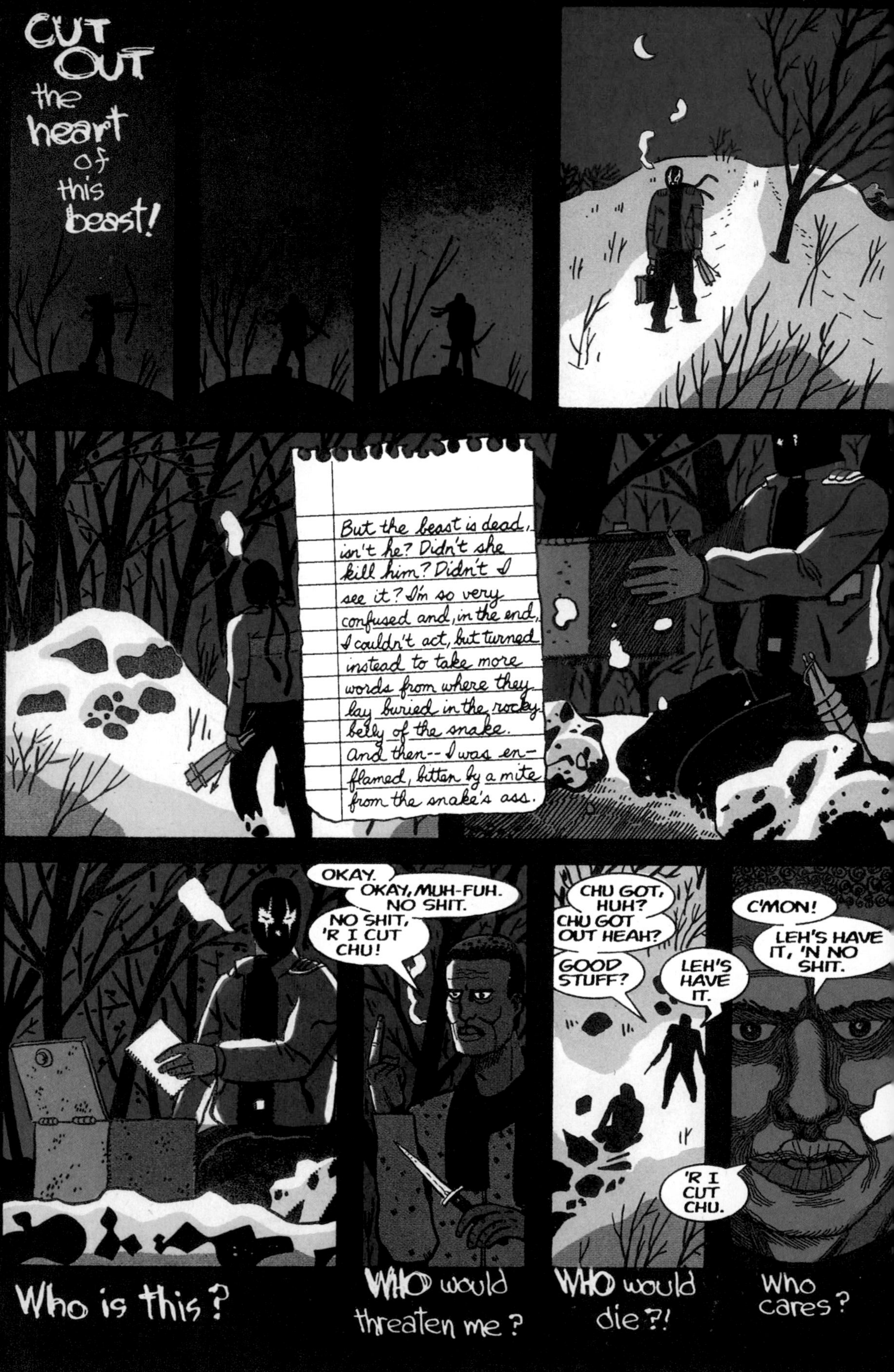
CUT OUT the heart of this beast!
But the beast is dead, isn't he? Didn't she kill him? Didn't I see it? I'm so very confused and, in the end, I couldn't act, but turned instead to take more words from where they lay buried in the rocky belly of the snake. And then-- I was enflamed, bitten by a mite from the snake's ass.
OKAY.
OKAY, MUH-FUH. NO SHIT.
NO SHIT, 'R I CUT CHU!
CHU GOT, HUH?
CHU GOT OUT HEAH?
GOOD STUFF?
LEH'S HAVE IT.
'R I CUT CHU.
C'MON!
LEH'S HAVE IT, 'N NO SHIT.
Who is this?
WHO would threaten me?
WHO would die?!
Who cares?

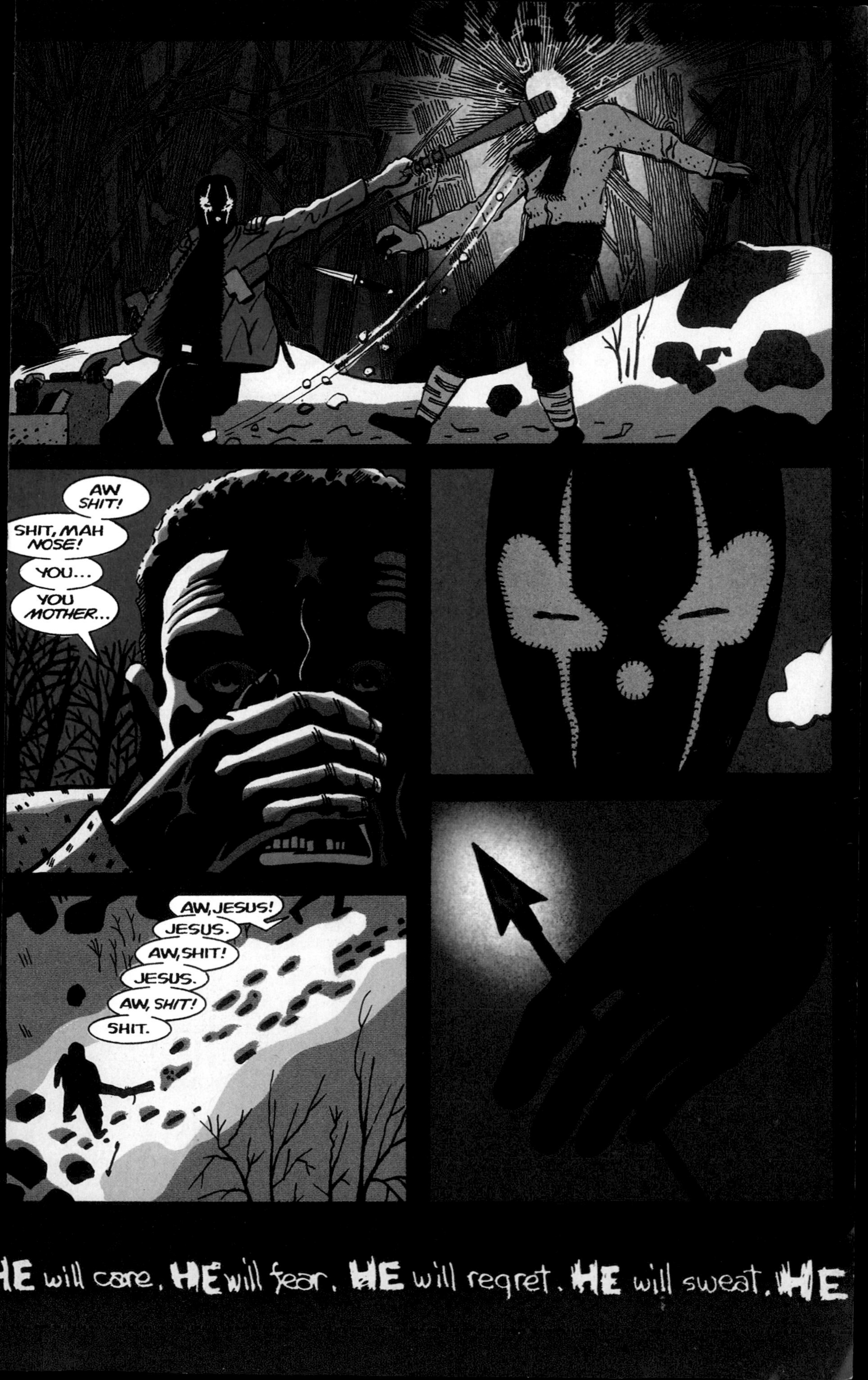
AW SHIT!
SHIT, MAH NOSE!
YOU...
YOU MOTHER...
AW, JESUS!
JESUS.
AW, SHIT!
JESUS.
AW, SHIT!
SHIT.
HE will care. HE will fear. HE will regret. HE will sweat. HE

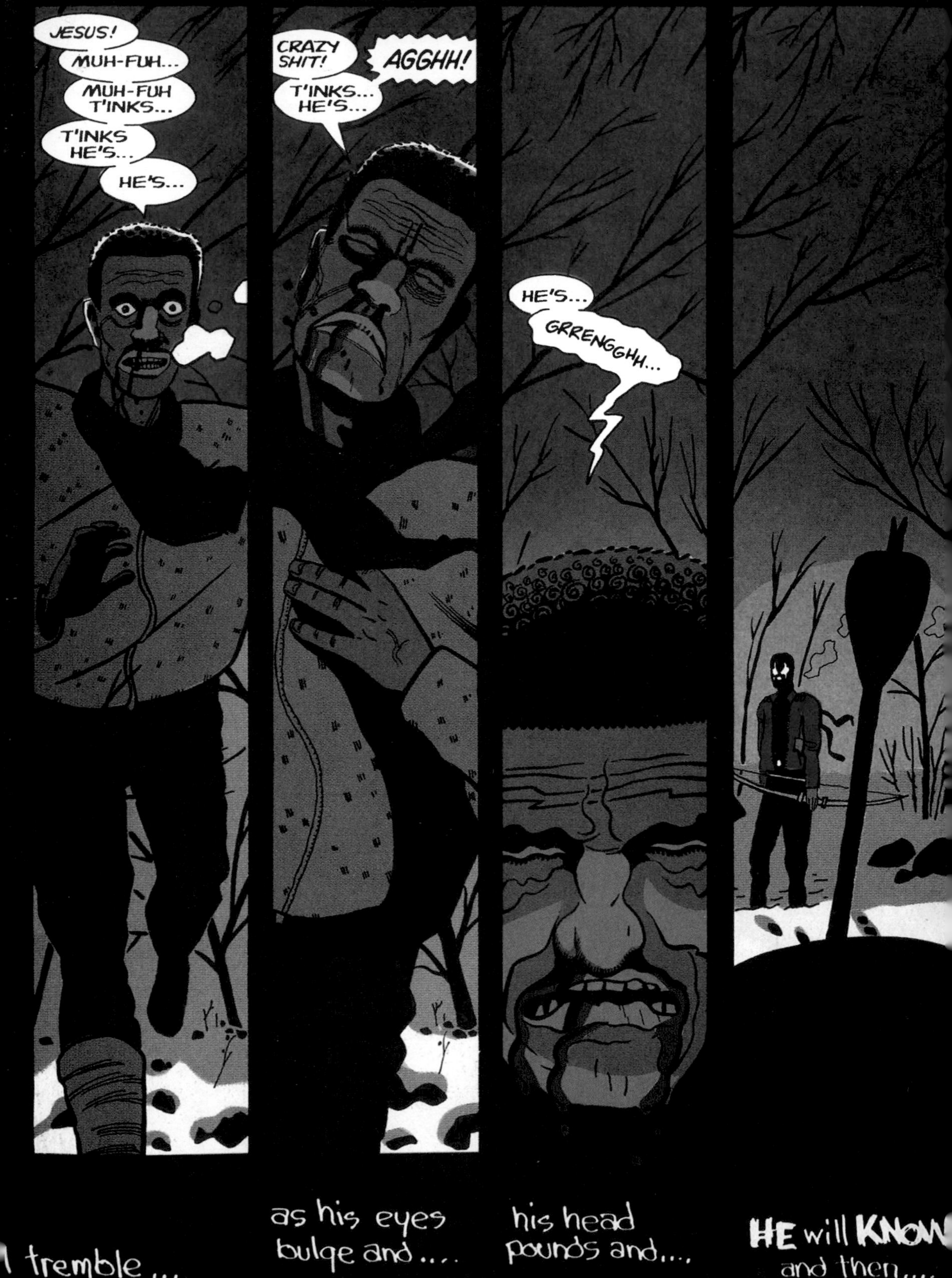
JESUS!
MUH-FUH...
MUH-FUH T'INKS...
T'INKS HE'S...
HE'S...
CRAZY SHIT!
T'INKS... HE'S...
AGGHH!
HE'S...
GRRENGGHH...
I tremble....
as his eyes bulge and....
his head pounds and....
HE will KNOW and then....

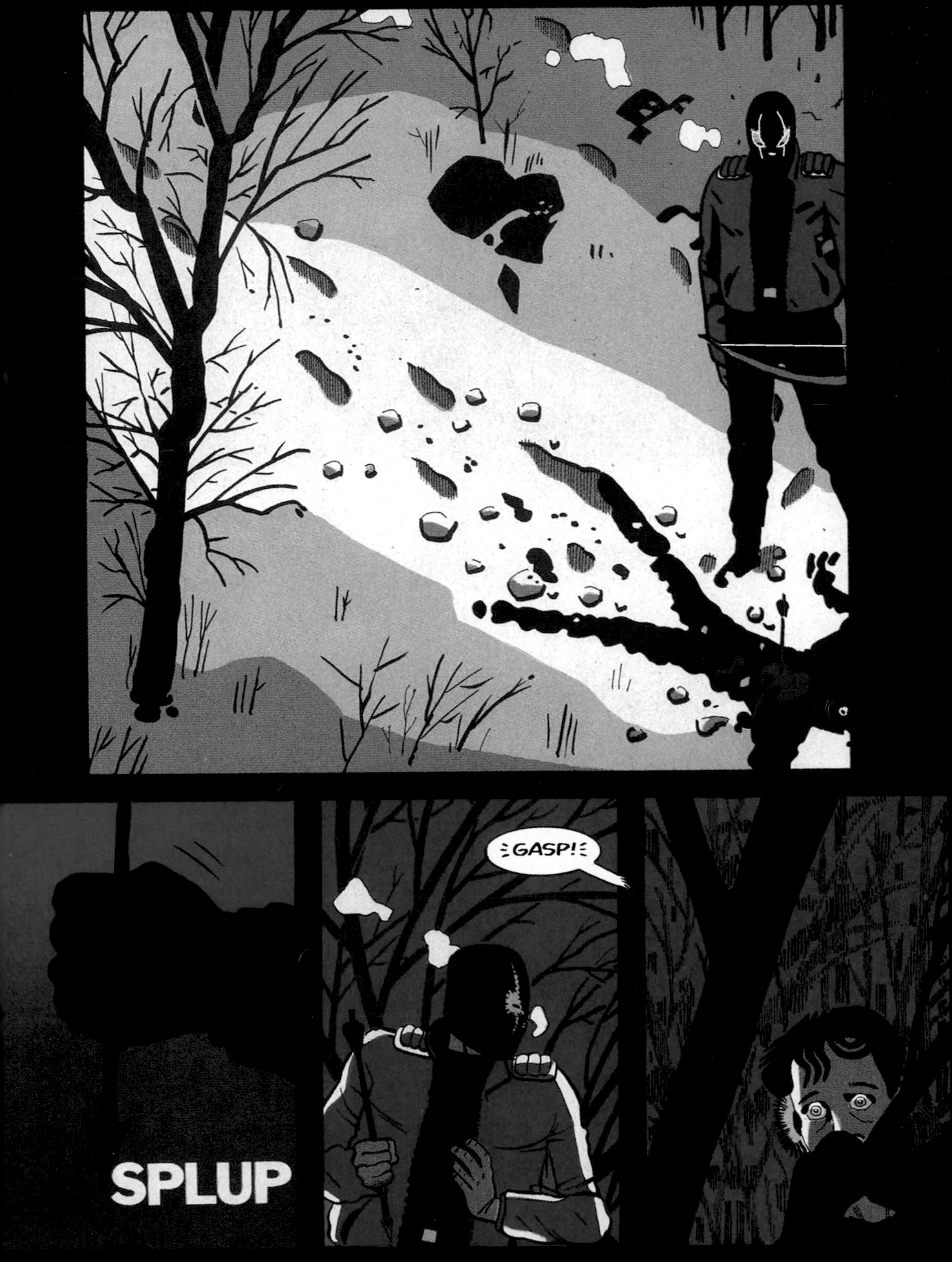
SPLUP
GASP!

Like all who would oppose me... All who would —

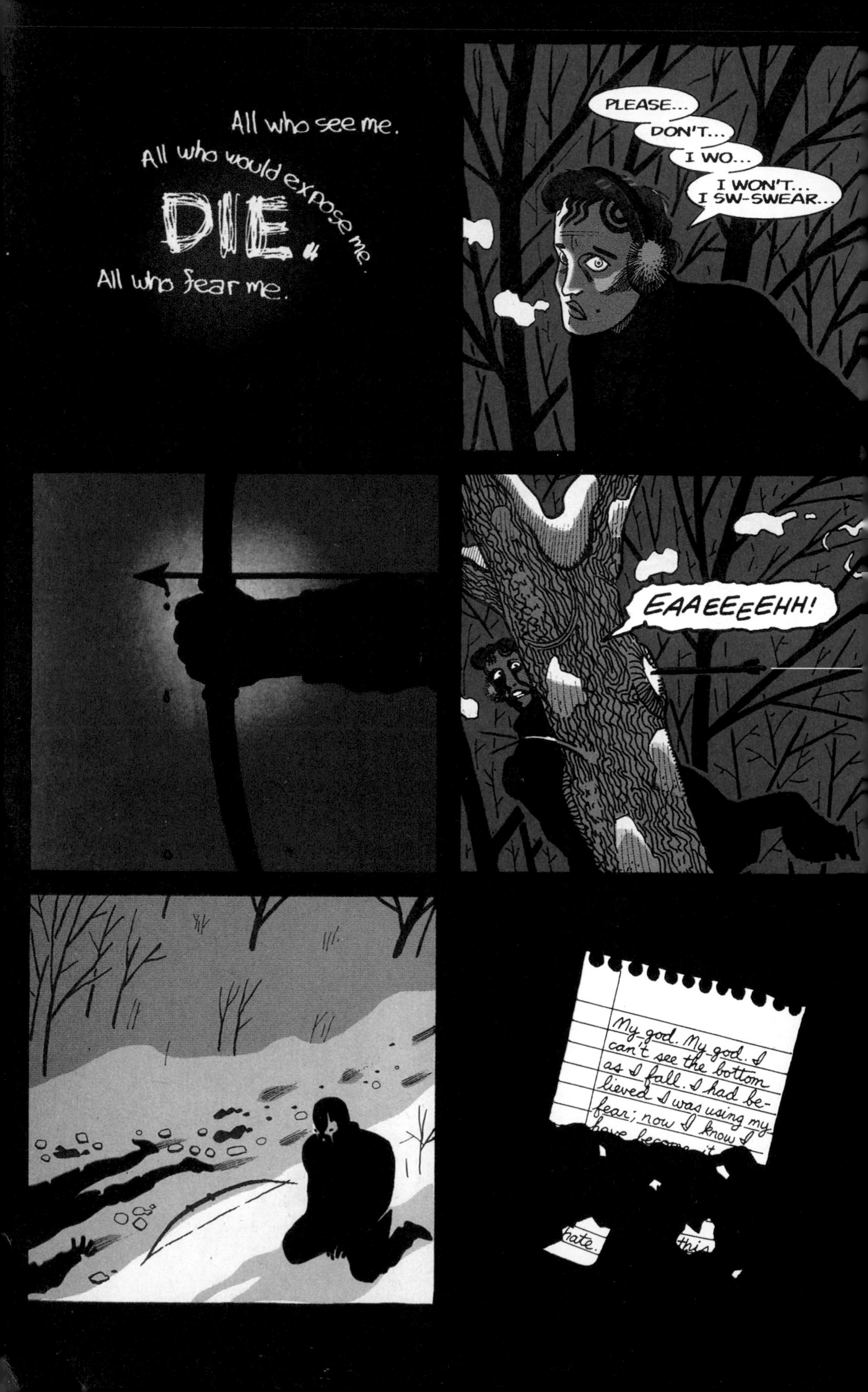
All who see me.
All who would expose me.
DIE.
All who fear me.
PLEASE...
DON'T...
I WO...
I WON'T... I SW-SWEAR...
EAAEEEEHH!
My god. My god. I can't see the bottom as I fall. I had believed I was using my fear; now I know I have become it
hate.
this

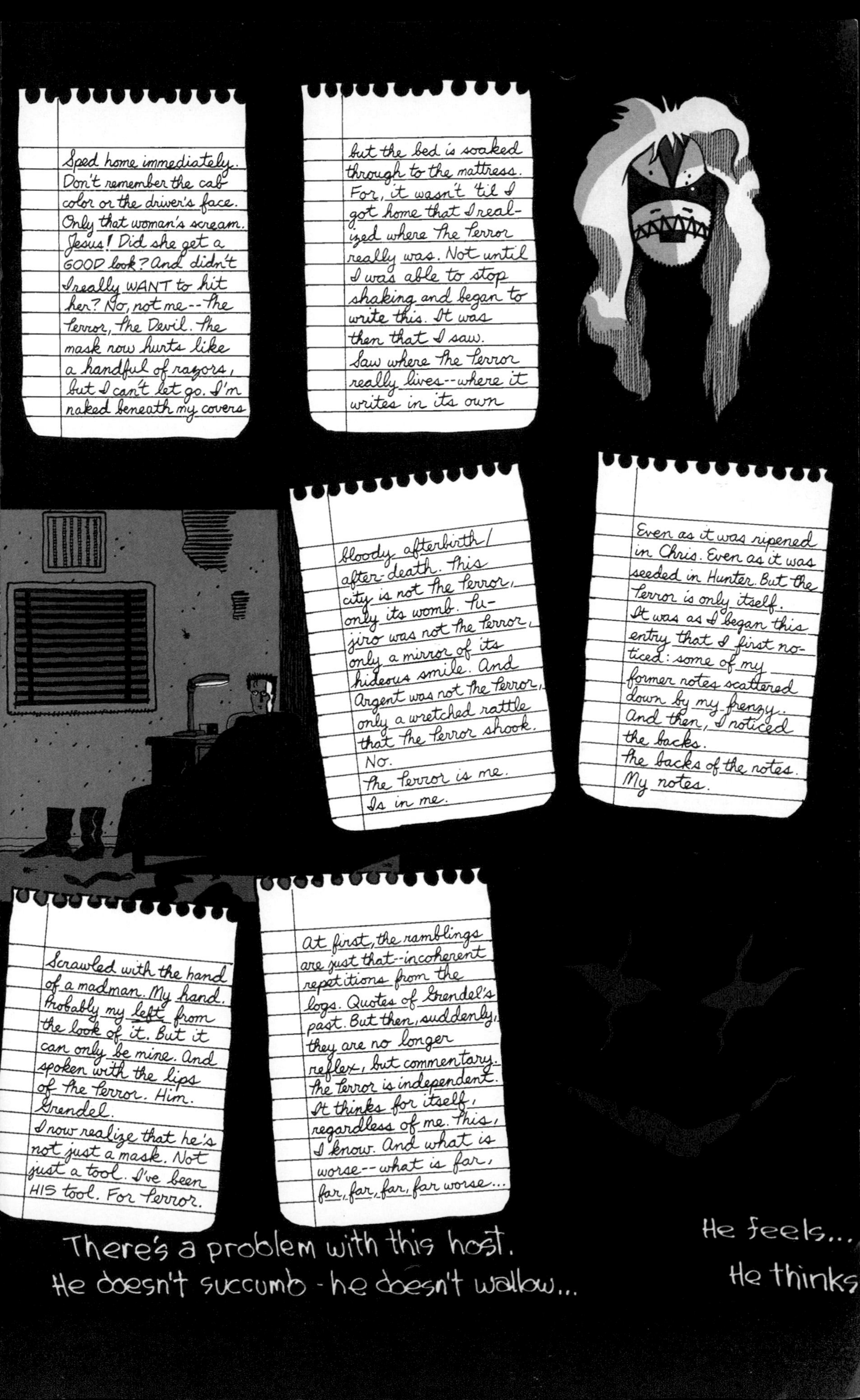
Sped home immediately. Don't remember the cab color or the driver's face. Only that woman's scream. Jesus! Did she get a GOOD look? And didn't I really WANT to hit her? No, not me--the Terror, the Devil. The mask now hurts like a handful of razors, but I can't let go. I'm naked beneath my covers
but the bed is soaked through to the mattress. For, it wasn't 'til I got home that I realized where the Terror really was. Not until I was able to stop shaking and began to write this. It was then that I saw. Saw where the Terror really lives--where it writes in its own
bloody afterbirth/after-death. This city is not the Terror, only its womb. Tujiro was not the Terror, only a mirror of its hideous smile. And Argent was not the Terror, only a wretched rattle that the Terror shook. No. The Terror is me. Is in me.
Even as it was ripened in Chris. Even as it was seeded in Hunter. But the Terror is only itself. It was as I began this entry that I first noticed: some of my former notes scattered down by my frenzy. And then, I noticed the backs. The backs of the notes. My notes.
Scrawled with the hand of a madman. My hand. Probably my left from the look of it. But it can only be mine. And spoken with the lips of the Terror. Him. Grendel. I now realize that he's not just a mask. Not just a tool. I've been HIS tool. For Terror.
At first, the ramblings are just that--incoherent repetitions from the logs. Quotes of Grendel's past. But then, suddenly, they are no longer reflex, but commentary. The Terror is independent. It thinks for itself, regardless of me. This, I know. And what is worse--what is far, far, far, far, far worse...
There's a problem with this host.
He doesn't succumb - he doesn't wallow...
He feels...
He thinks

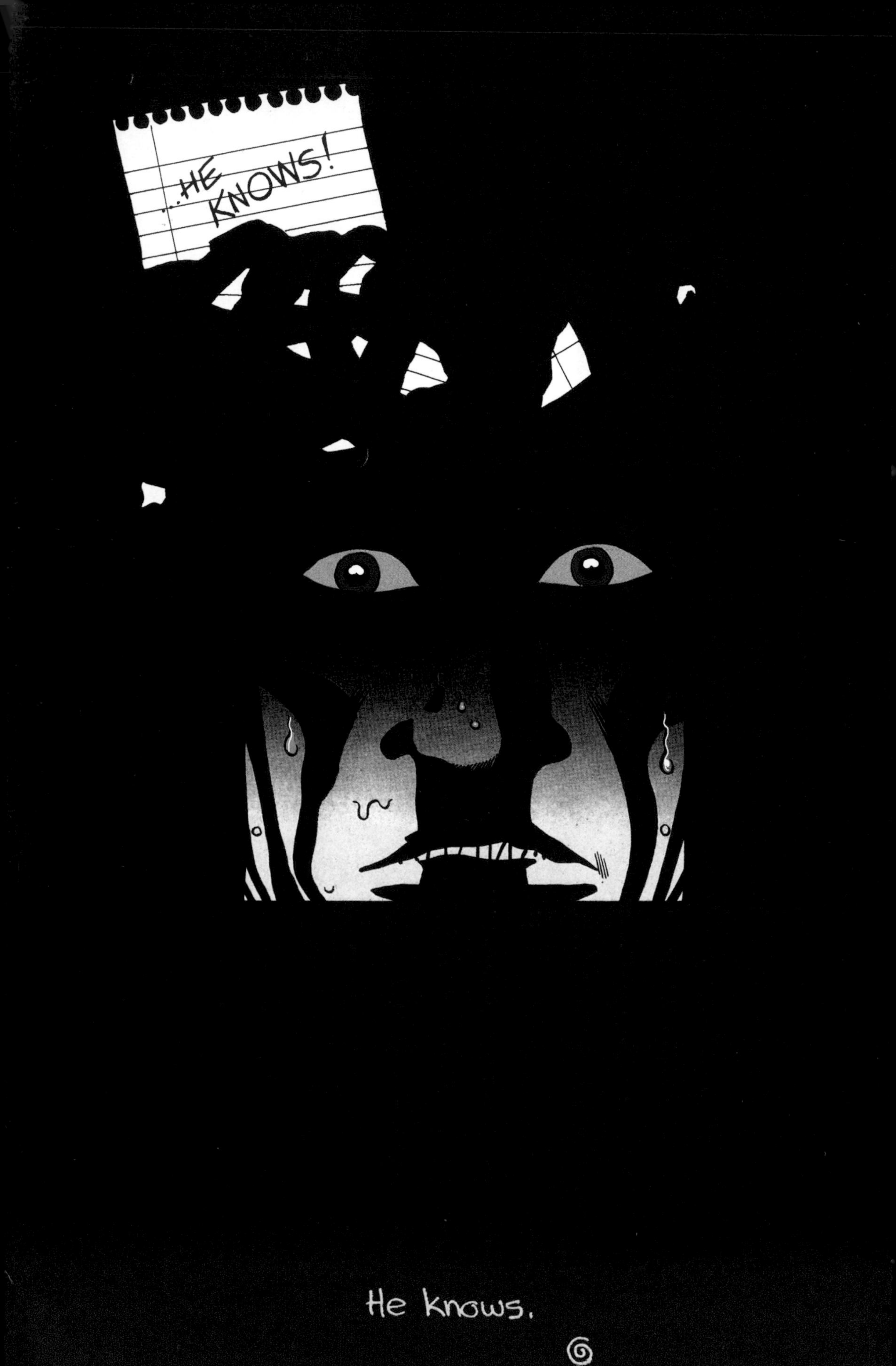
...HE KNOWS!
He knows.

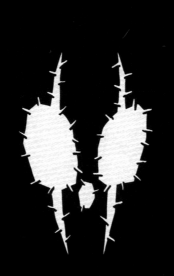

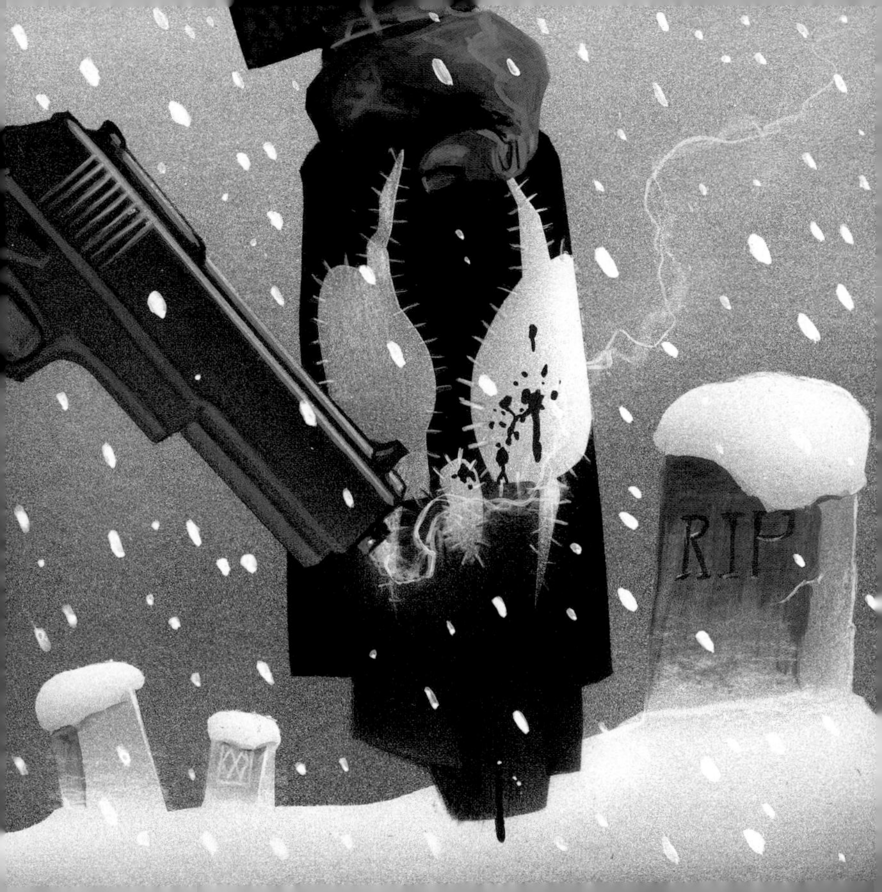
RIP

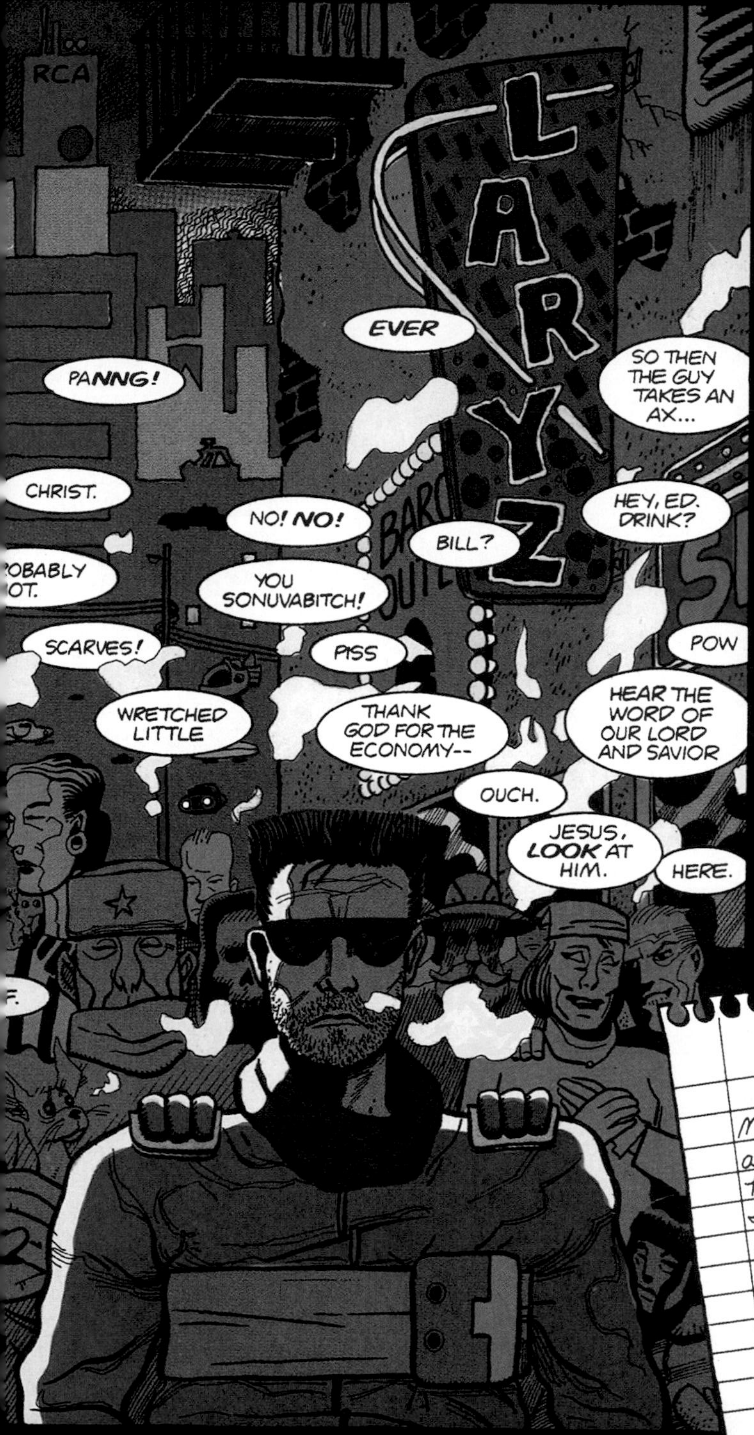
RCA
L A R Y Z
EVER
PANNG!
SO THEN THE GUY TAKES AN AX...
CHRIST.
NO! NO!
BILL?
HEY, ED. DRINK?
ROBABLY OT.
YOU SONUVABITCH!
SCARVES!
PISS
POW
WRETCHED LITTLE
THANK GOD FOR THE ECONOMY--
HEAR THE WORD OF OUR LORD AND SAVIOR
OUCH.
JESUS, LOOK AT HIM.
HERE.

BEAT THE DEVIL

THIRD PART.

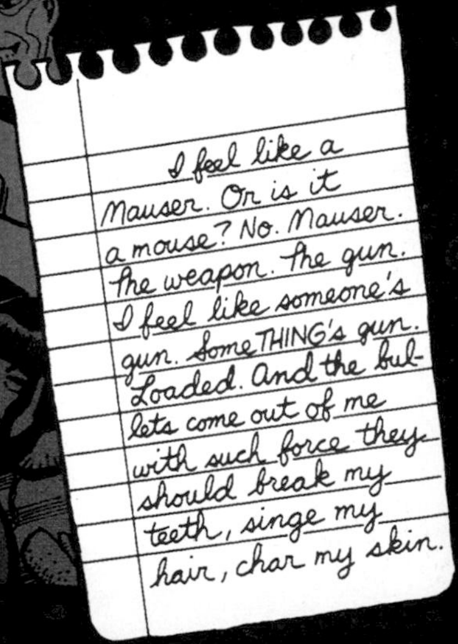
I feel like a Mauser. Or is it a mouse? No. Mauser. The weapon. The gun. I feel like someone's gun. SomeTHING's gun. Loaded. And the bullets come out of me with such force they should break my teeth, singe my hair, char my skin.

...ven the correct target, the accuracy, and, of course, the right weapon... one can accomplish much.

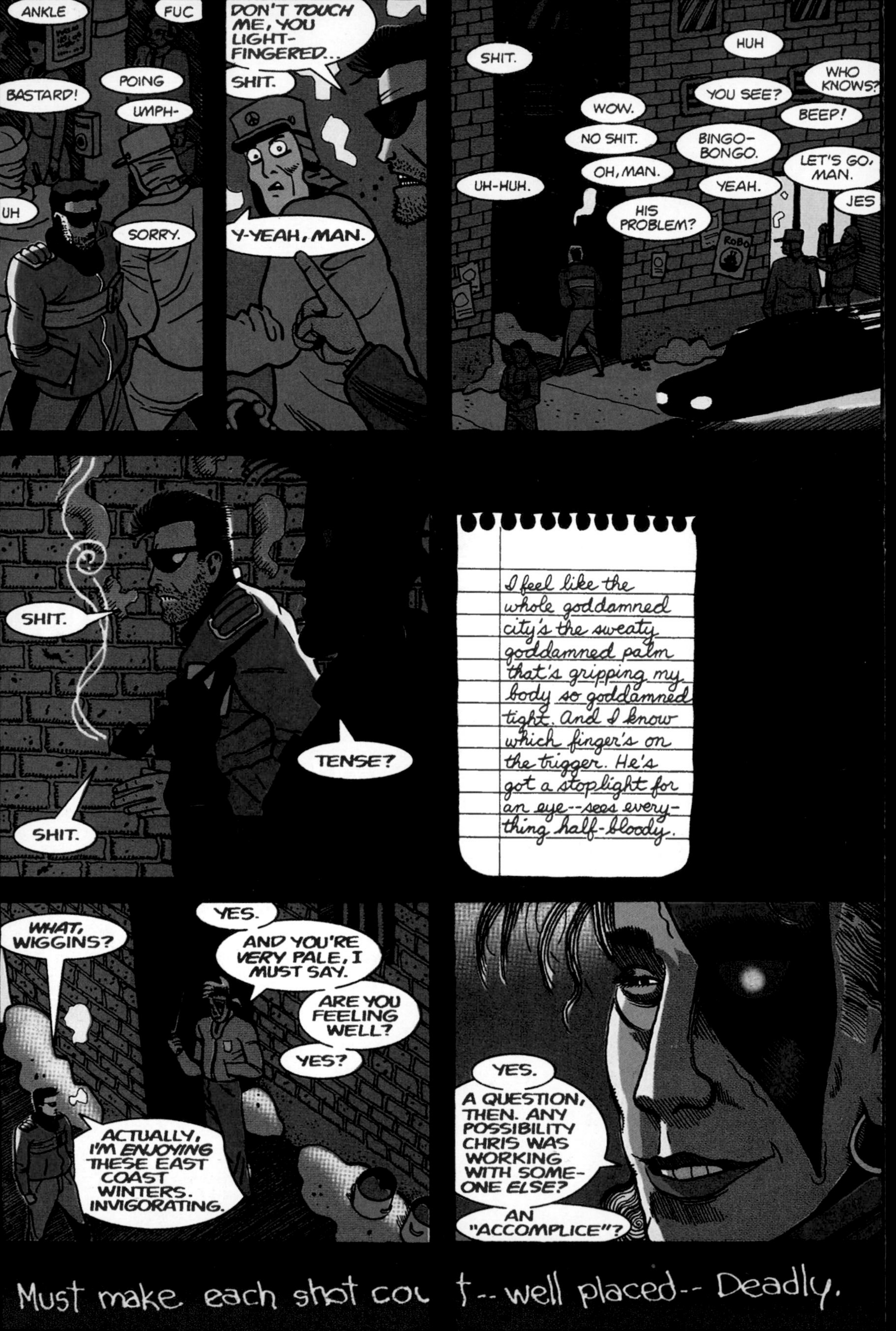
ANKLE
FUC
BASTARD!
POING
UMPH-
UH
SORRY.
DON'T TOUCH ME, YOU LIGHT-FINGERED...
SHIT.
Y-YEAH, MAN.
SHIT.
HUH
WHO KNOWS?
YOU SEE?
WOW.
BEEP!
NO SHIT.
BINGO-BONGO.
LET'S GO, MAN.
OH, MAN.
UH-HUH.
YEAH.
JES
HIS PROBLEM?
SHIT.
TENSE?
SHIT.
I feel like the whole goddamned city's the sweaty goddamned palm that's gripping my body so goddamned tight. And I know which finger's on the trigger. He's got a stoplight for an eye--sees every-thing half-bloody.
WHAT, WIGGINS?
YES.
AND YOU'RE VERY PALE, I MUST SAY.
ARE YOU FEELING WELL?
YES?
ACTUALLY, I'M ENJOYING THESE EAST COAST WINTERS. INVIGORATING.
YES.
A QUESTION, THEN. ANY POSSIBILITY CHRIS WAS WORKING WITH SOME-ONE ELSE?
AN "ACCOMPLICE"?
Must make each shot cou t-- well placed-- Deadly.

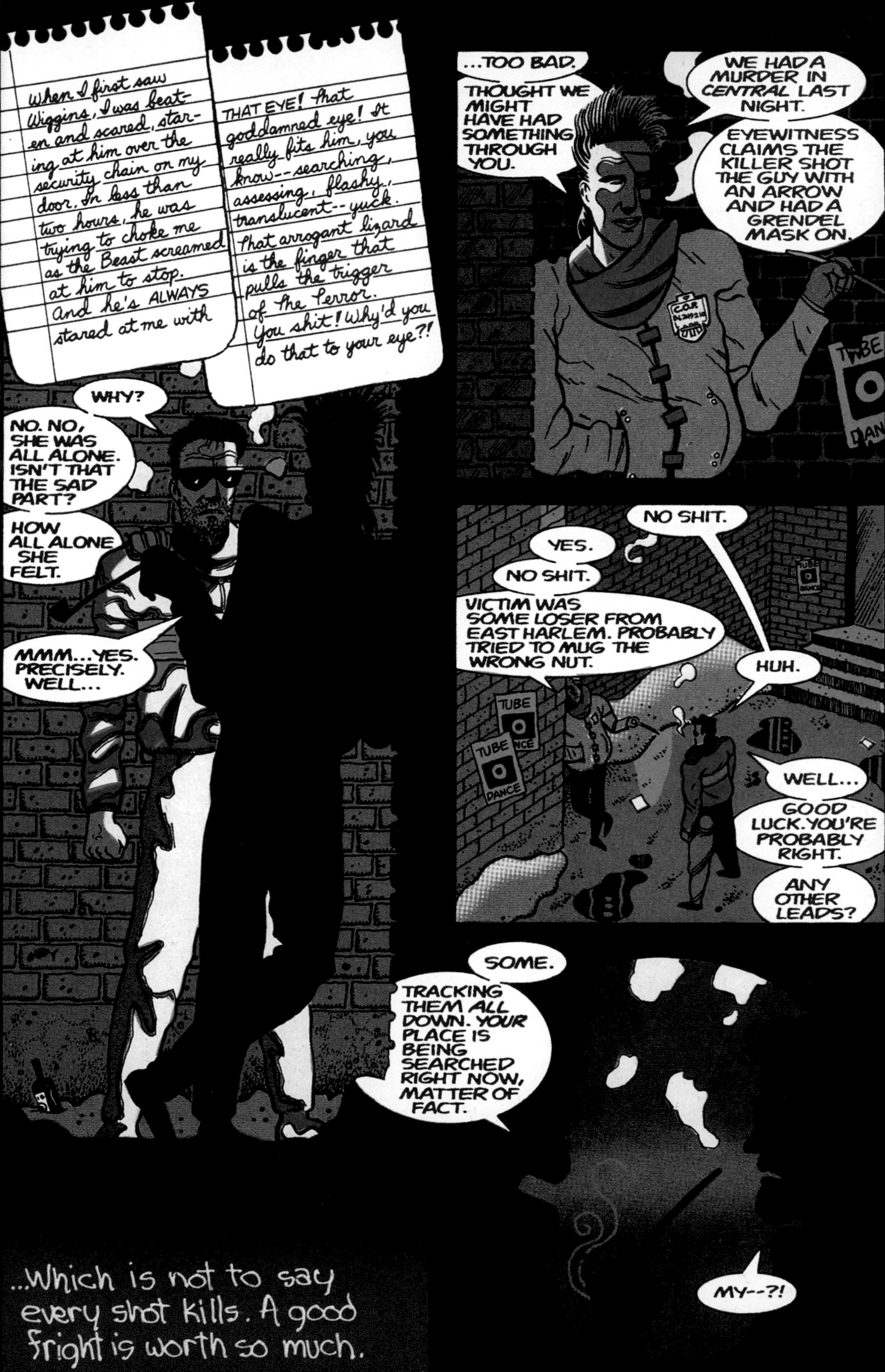
When I first saw Wiggins, I was beaten and scared, staring at him over the security chain on my door. In less than two hours, he was trying to choke me as the Beast screamed at him to stop. And he's ALWAYS stared at me with
THAT EYE! that goddamned eye! It really fits him, you know--searching, assessing, flashy, translucent--yuck. That arrogant lizard is the finger that pulls the trigger of the Terror. You shit! Why'd you do that to your eye?!
...TOO BAD.
THOUGHT WE MIGHT HAVE HAD SOMETHING THROUGH YOU.
WE HAD A MURDER IN CENTRAL LAST NIGHT.
EYEWITNESS CLAIMS THE KILLER SHOT THE GUY WITH AN ARROW AND HAD A GRENDEL MASK ON.
WHY?
NO. NO, SHE WAS ALL ALONE. ISN'T THAT THE SAD PART?
HOW ALL ALONE SHE FELT.
MMM...YES. PRECISELY. WELL...
NO SHIT.
YES.
NO SHIT.
VICTIM WAS SOME LOSER FROM EAST HARLEM. PROBABLY TRIED TO MUG THE WRONG NUT.
HUH.
WELL...
GOOD LUCK. YOU'RE PROBABLY RIGHT.
ANY OTHER LEADS?
SOME.
TRACKING THEM ALL DOWN. YOUR PLACE IS BEING SEARCHED RIGHT NOW, MATTER OF FACT.
MY--?!
...Which is not to say every shot kills. A good fright is worth so much.

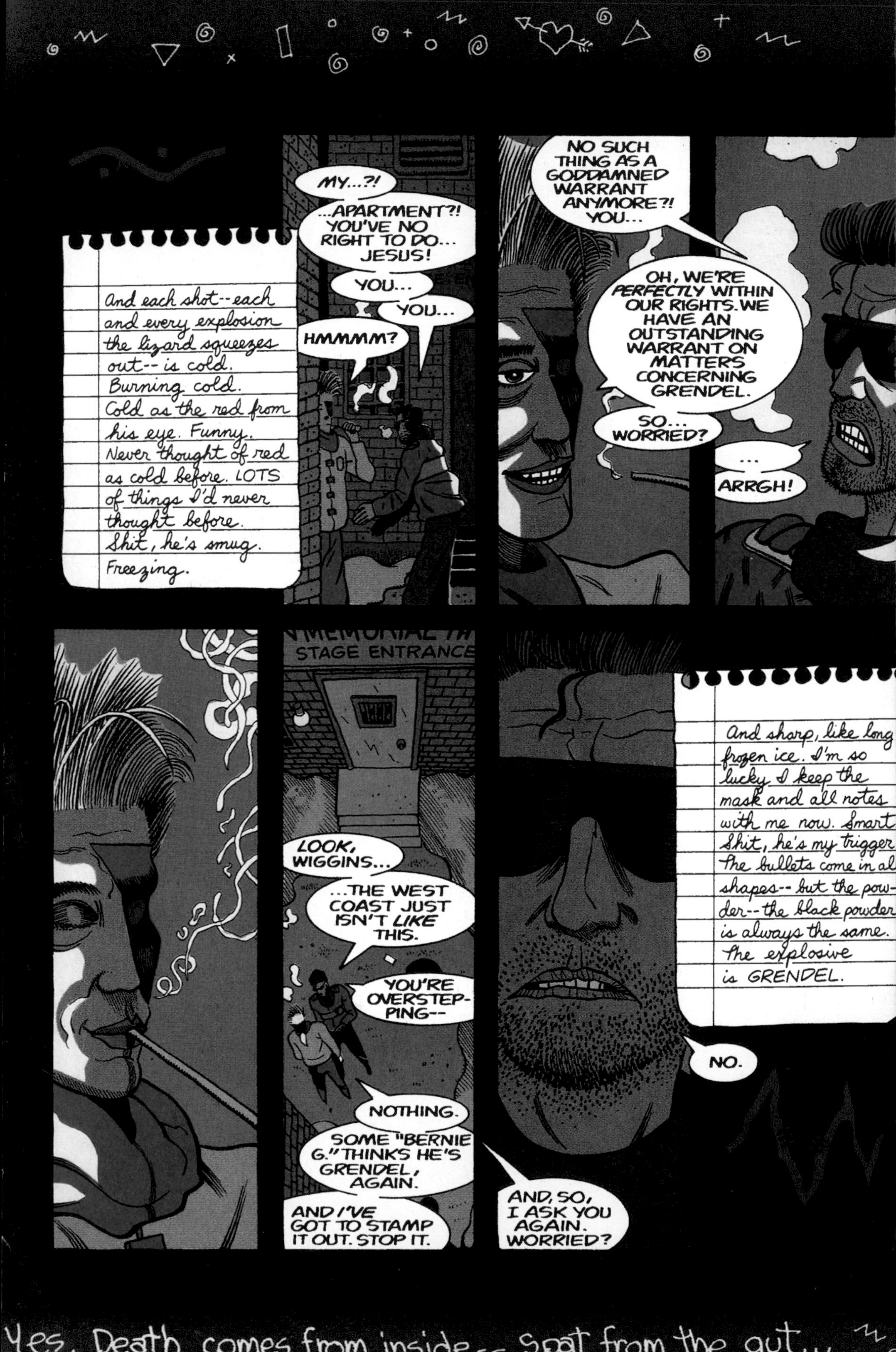
And each shot--each and every explosion the lizard squeezes out-- is cold. Burning cold. Cold as the red from his eye. Funny. Never thought of red as cold before. LOTS of things I'd never thought before. Shit, he's smug. Freezing.
MY...?!
...APARTMENT?! YOU'VE NO RIGHT TO DO... JESUS!
YOU...
YOU...
HMMMM?
NO SUCH THING AS A GODDAMNED WARRANT ANYMORE?! YOU...
OH, WE'RE PERFECTLY WITHIN OUR RIGHTS. WE HAVE AN OUTSTANDING WARRANT ON MATTERS CONCERNING GRENDEL.
SO... WORRIED?
...
ARRGH!
STAGE ENTRANCE
LOOK, WIGGINS...
...THE WEST COAST JUST ISN'T LIKE THIS.
YOU'RE OVERSTEPPING--
NOTHING.
SOME "BERNIE G." THINKS HE'S GRENDEL, AGAIN.
AND I'VE GOT TO STAMP IT OUT. STOP IT.
And sharp, like long frozen ice. I'm so lucky I keep the mask and all notes with me now. Smart. Shit, he's my trigger. The bullets come in all shapes-- but the powder--the black powder is always the same. The explosive is GRENDEL.
NO.
AND, SO, I ASK YOU AGAIN. WORRIED?
Yes. Death comes from inside-- spat from the gut...

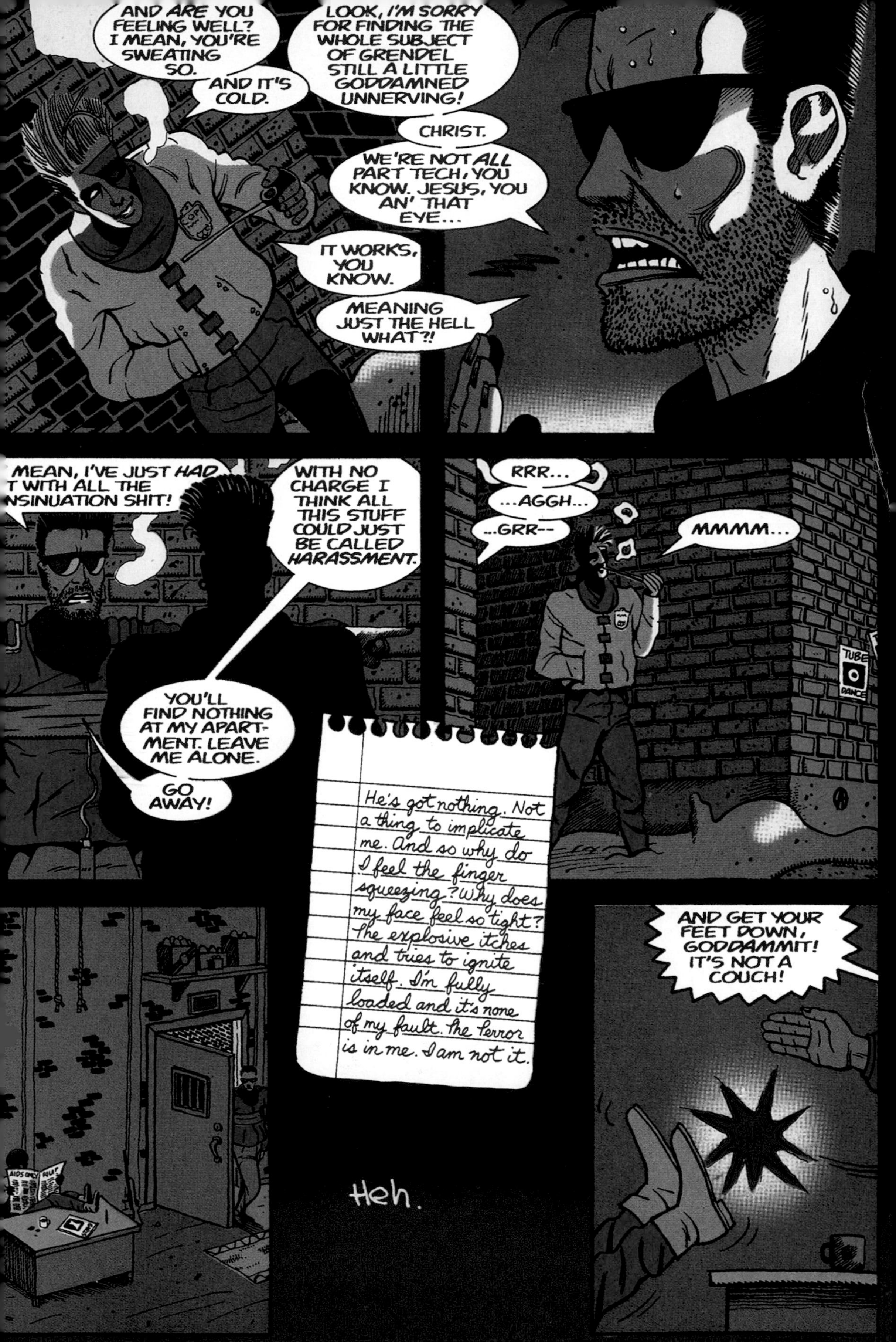
AND ARE YOU FEELING WELL? I MEAN, YOU'RE SWEATING SO.
AND IT'S COLD.
LOOK, I'M SORRY FOR FINDING THE WHOLE SUBJECT OF GRENDEL STILL A LITTLE GODDAMNED UNNERVING!
CHRIST.
WE'RE NOT ALL PART TECH, YOU KNOW. JESUS, YOU AN' THAT EYE...
IT WORKS, YOU KNOW.
MEANING JUST THE HELL WHAT?!
MEAN, I'VE JUST HAD T WITH ALL THE NSINUATION SHIT!
WITH NO CHARGE I THINK ALL THIS STUFF COULD JUST BE CALLED HARASSMENT.
YOU'LL FIND NOTHING AT MY APARTMENT. LEAVE ME ALONE.
GO AWAY!
RRR...
...AGGH...
...GRR--
MMMM...
TUBE
DANCE
He's got nothing. Not a thing to implicate me. And so why do I feel the finger squeezing? Why does my face feel so tight? The explosive itches and tries to ignite itself. I'm fully loaded and it's none of my fault. The terror is in me. I am not it.
Heh.
AND GET YOUR FEET DOWN, GODDAMMIT! IT'S NOT A COUCH!

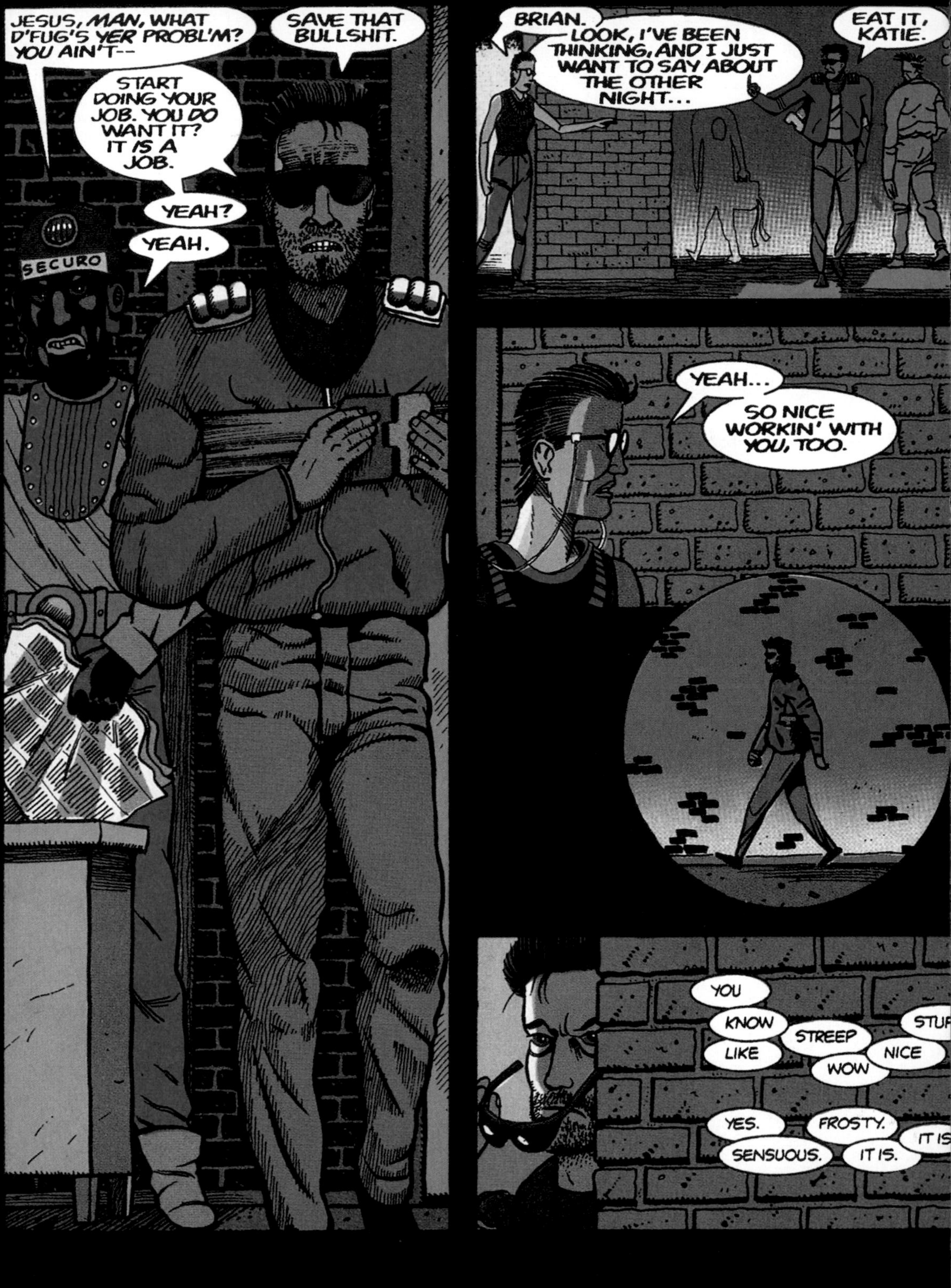
JESUS, MAN, WHAT D'FUG'S YER PROBL'M? YOU AIN'T--
SAVE THAT BULLSHIT.
START DOING YOUR JOB. YOU DO WANT IT? IT IS A JOB.
YEAH?
YEAH.
SECURO
BRIAN.
LOOK, I'VE BEEN THINKING, AND I JUST WANT TO SAY ABOUT THE OTHER NIGHT...
EAT IT, KATIE.
YEAH...
SO NICE WORKIN' WITH YOU, TOO.
YOU
KNOW
LIKE
STREEP
WOW
NICE
YES.
FROSTY.
SENSUOUS.
IT IS.

And of course the truest weapon is one's self... all els
extension.

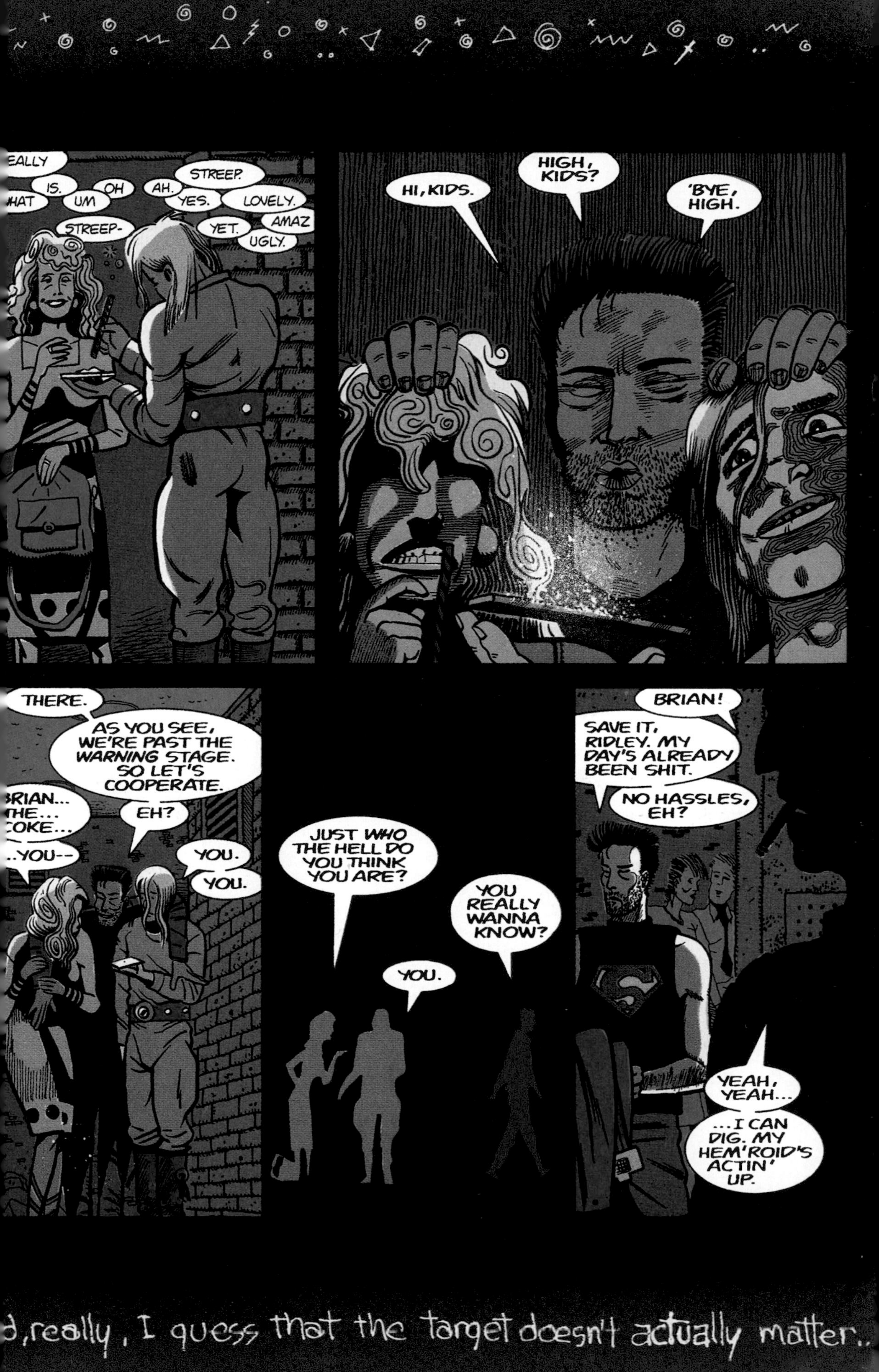
EALLY
HAT
IS.
UM
OH
AH.
STREEP.
YES.
LOVELY.
STREEP-
YET.
AMAZ
UGLY.
HI, KIDS.
HIGH, KIDS?
'BYE, HIGH.
THERE.
AS YOU SEE, WE'RE PAST THE WARNING STAGE. SO LET'S COOPERATE.
BRIAN... THE... COKE...
EH?
..YOU--
YOU.
YOU.
JUST WHO THE HELL DO YOU THINK YOU ARE?
YOU REALLY WANNA KNOW?
YOU.
BRIAN!
SAVE IT, RIDLEY. MY DAY'S ALREADY BEEN SHIT.
NO HASSLES, EH?
YEAH, YEAH...
...I CAN DIG. MY HEM'ROID'S ACTIN' UP.
d, really, I guess that the target doesn't actually matter...

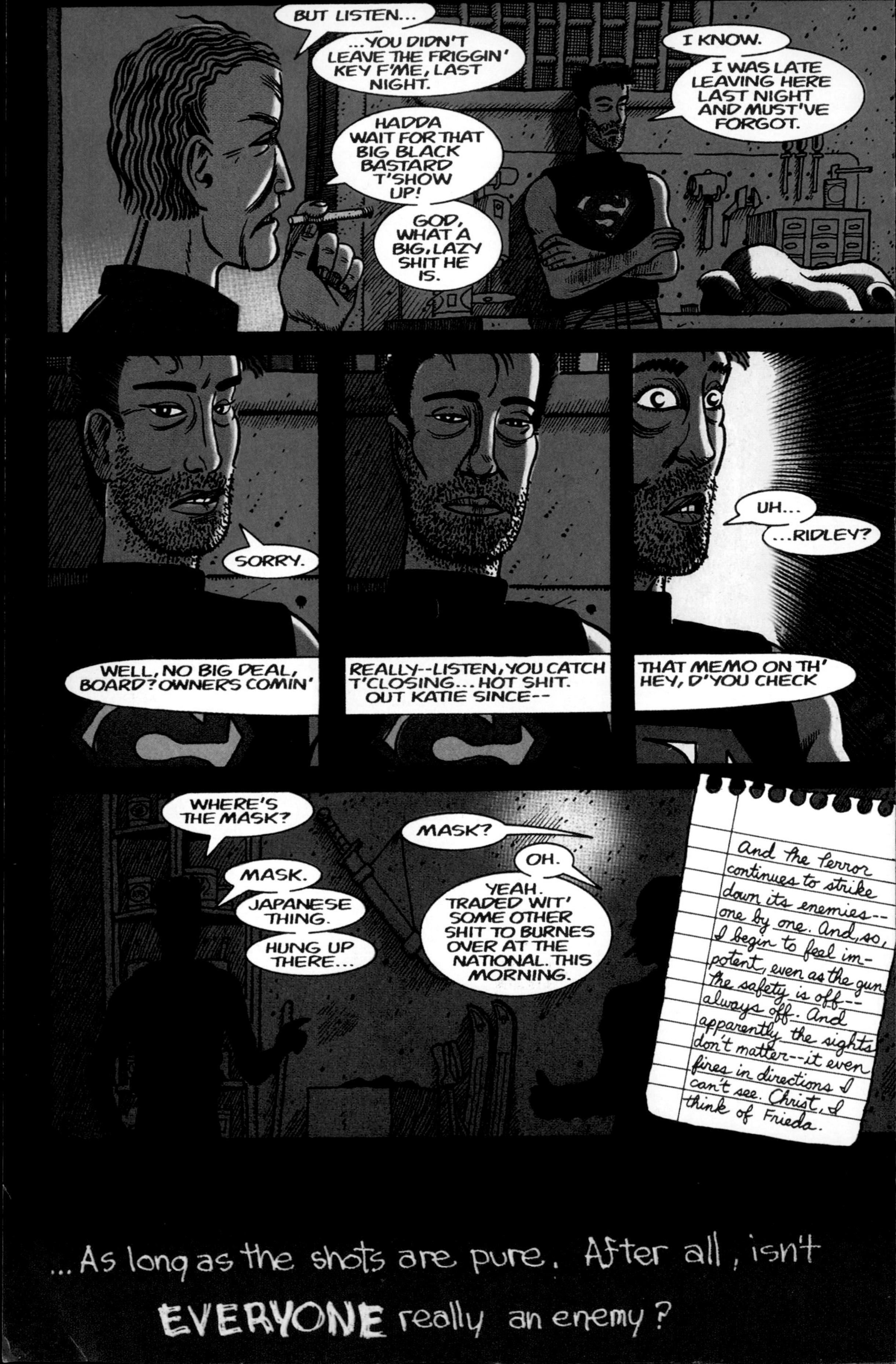
BUT LISTEN...
...YOU DIDN'T LEAVE THE FRIGGIN' KEY F'ME, LAST NIGHT.
I KNOW.
I WAS LATE LEAVING HERE LAST NIGHT AND MUST'VE FORGOT.
HADDA WAIT FOR THAT BIG BLACK BASTARD T'SHOW UP!
GOD, WHAT A BIG, LAZY SHIT HE IS.
SORRY.
WELL, NO BIG DEAL, BOARD? OWNER'S COMIN'
REALLY--LISTEN, YOU CATCH T'CLOSING... HOT SHIT. OUT KATIE SINCE--
UH...
...RIDLEY?
THAT MEMO ON TH' HEY, D'YOU CHECK
WHERE'S THE MASK?
MASK?
MASK.
JAPANESE THING.
HUNG UP THERE...
OH.
YEAH. TRADED WIT' SOME OTHER SHIT TO BURNES OVER AT THE NATIONAL. THIS MORNING.
And the terror continues to strike down its enemies--one by one. And, so, I begin to feel impotent, even as the gun. The safety is off--always off. And apparently the sights don't matter--it even fires in directions I can't see. Christ, I think of Frieda.
...As long as the shots are pure. After all, isn't
EVERYONE really an enemy?

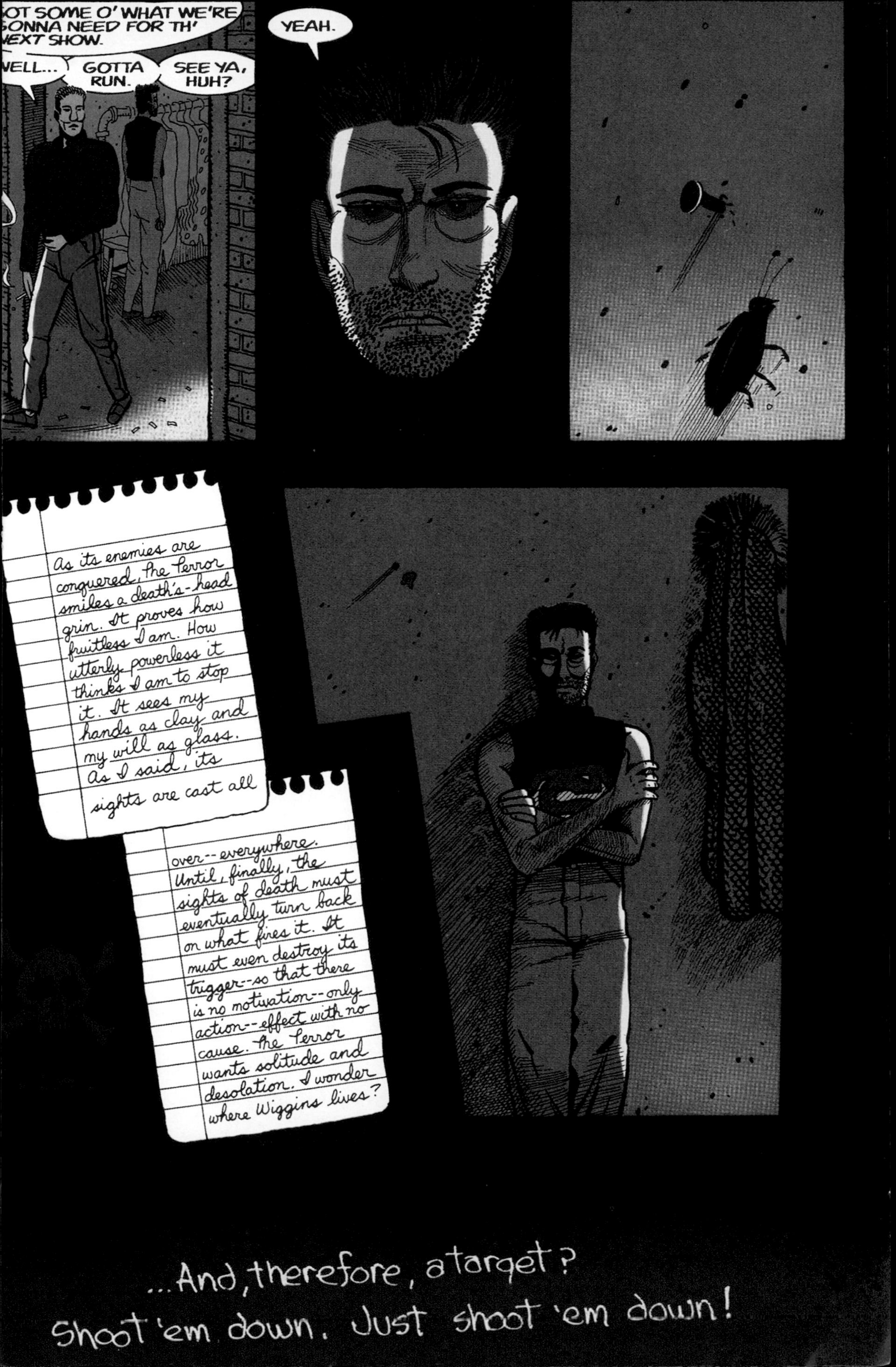
OT SOME O' WHAT WE'RE GONNA NEED FOR TH' NEXT SHOW.
YEAH.
WELL...
GOTTA RUN.
SEE YA, HUH?
As its enemies are conquered, the Terror smiles a death's-head grin. It proves how fruitless I am. How utterly powerless it thinks I am to stop it. It sees my hands as clay and my will as glass. As I said, its sights are cast all
over--everywhere. Until, finally, the sights of death must eventually turn back on what fires it. It must even destroy its trigger--so that there is no motivation--only action--effect with no cause. The Terror wants solitude and desolation. I wonder where Wiggins lives?
...And, therefore, a target?
Shoot 'em down. Just shoot 'em down!

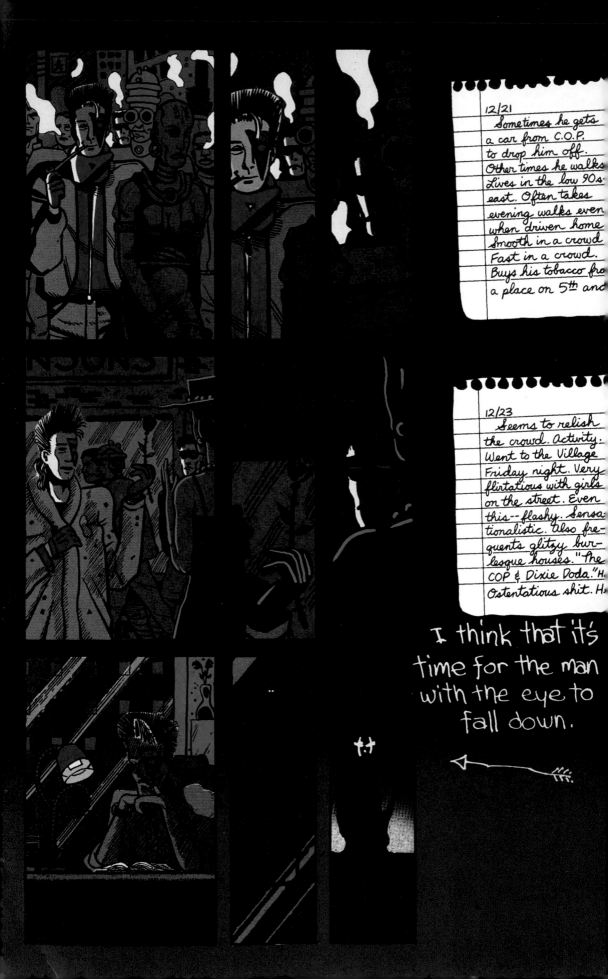

12/21
Sometimes he gets a car from C.O.P. to drop him off. Other times he walks. Lives in the low 90s east. Often takes evening walks even when driven home. Smooth in a crowd. Fast in a crowd. Buys his tobacco fro a place on 5th and

12/23
Seems to relish the crowd. Activity: Went to the Village Friday night. Very flirtatious with girls on the street. Even this--flashy. Sensationalistic. Also frequents glitzy burlesque houses. "The COP & Dixie Doda." H Ostentatious shit. H

I think that it's time for the man with the eye to fall down.

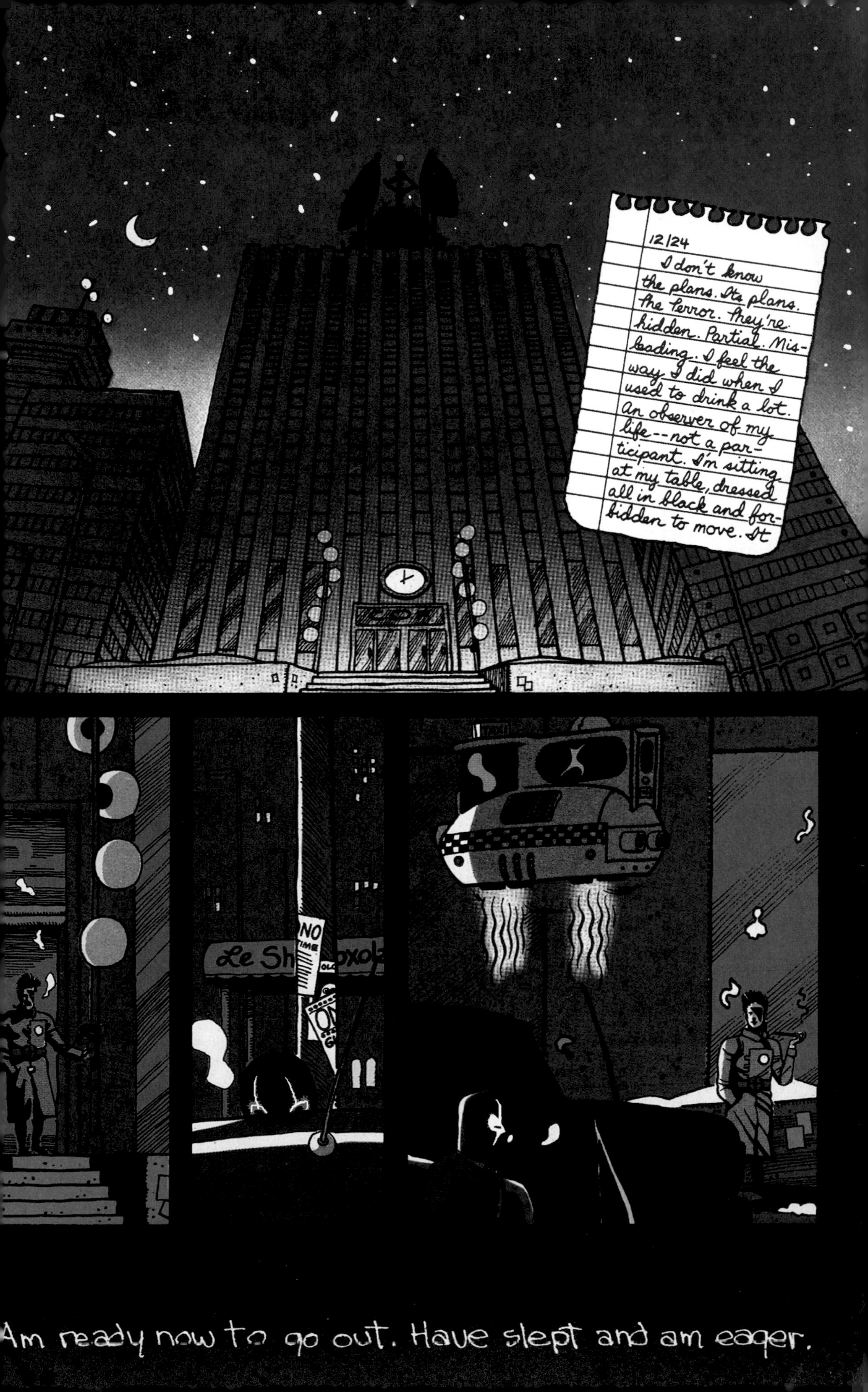
12/24
I don't know the plans. Its plans. The terror. They're hidden. Partial. Mis-leading. I feel the way I did when I used to drink a lot. An observer of my life--not a par-ticipant. I'm sitting at my table, dressed all in black and for-bidden to move. It
Le Sh
Am ready now to go out. Have slept and am eager.

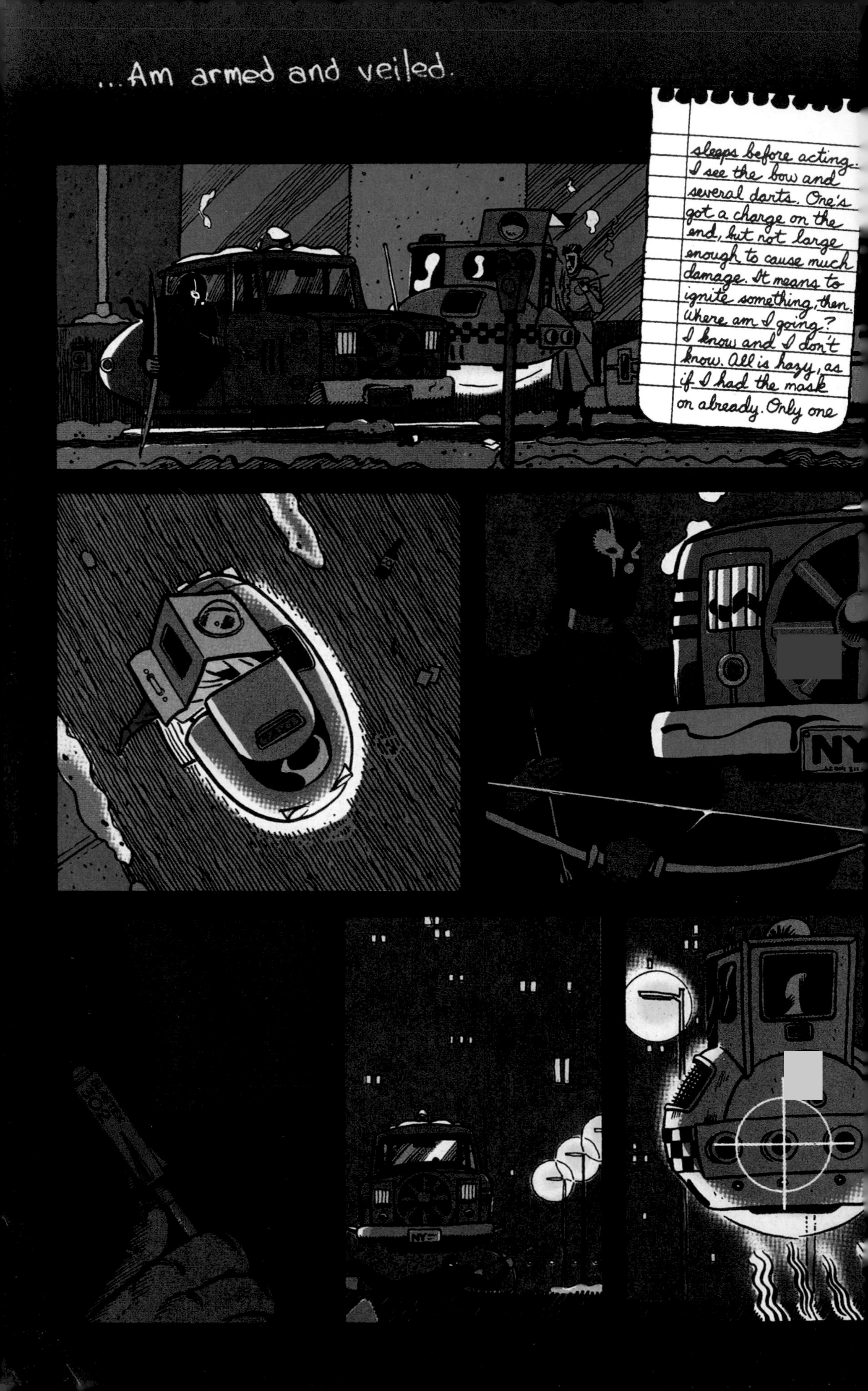
...Am armed and veiled.
sleeps before acting. I see the bow and several darts. One's got a charge on the end, but not large enough to cause much damage. It means to ignite something, then. Where am I going? I know and I don't know. All is hazy, as if I had the mask on already. Only one
NY
NY

Haven't yet decided on the order of things.
How quick?

pop!

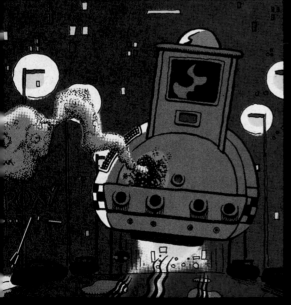 

charge. The others are
back-ups? It is de-
termined. It is con-
fident even in its de-
ficiencies. And it is
ruthless.
Oh, GOD! I don't
want to do this.

Yes. I do.
Don't I?
Aren't I?
Am I?

Depends on what opportunities
present themselves. A bang up the
ass, maybe?
...Maybe.

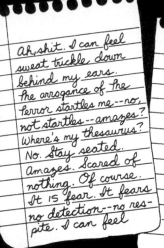

Ah, shit. I can feel sweat trickle down behind my ears. The arrogance of the Terror startles me--no, not startles--amazes? Where's my thesaurus? No. Stay seated. Amazes. Scared of nothing. Of course. It is fear. It fears no detection--no respite. I can feel

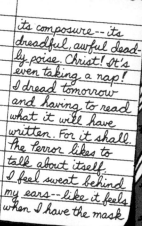

its composure-- its dreadful, awful deadly poise. Christ! It's even taking a nap! I dread tomorrow and having to read what it will have written. For it shall. The Terror likes to talk about itself. I feel sweat behind my ears--like it feels when I have the mask

We'll see.

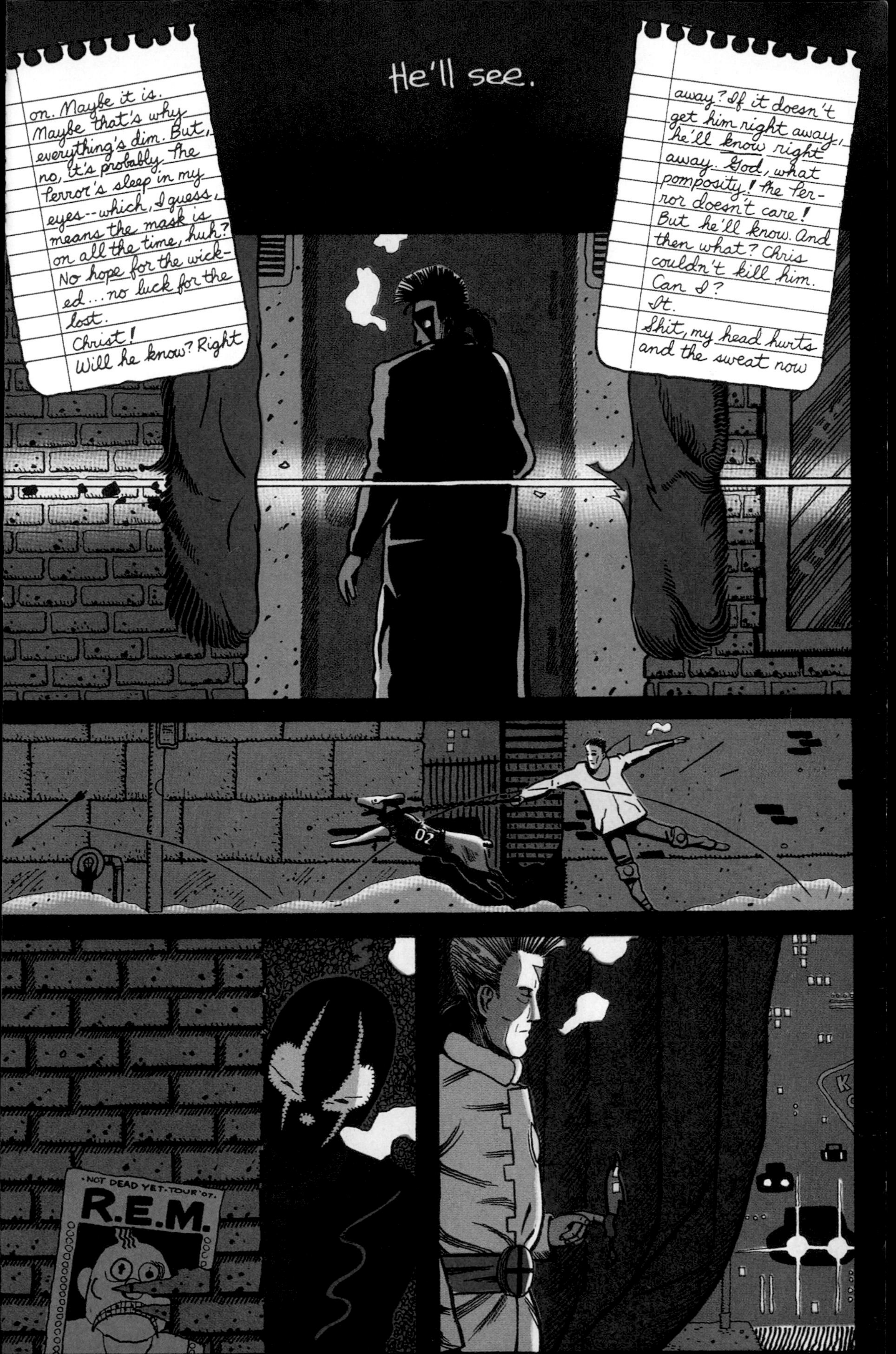
on. Maybe it is. Maybe that's why everything's dim. But, no, it's probably the Terror's sleep in my eyes--which, I guess, means the mask is on all the time, huh? No hope for the wicked...no luck for the lost.
Christ!
Will he know? Right
He'll see.
away? If it doesn't get him right away, he'll know right away. God, what pomposity! The Terror doesn't care! But he'll know. And then what? Chris couldn't kill him. Can I?
It.
Shit, my head hurts and the sweat now
20
NOT DEAD YET TOUR '07
R.E.M.

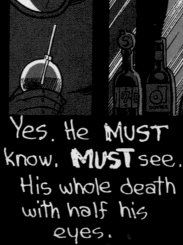

Yes. He **MUST** know. **MUST** see. His whole death with half his eyes.

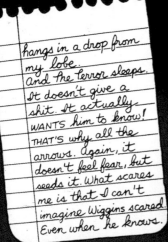

hangs in a drop from my lobe.
And the terror sleeps. It doesn't give a shit. It actually WANTS him to know! THAT'S why all the arrows. Again, it doesn't feel fear, but seeds it. What scares me is that I can't imagine Wiggins scared. Even when he knows.

It's sleeping to
gather energy. A wave
approaches. A tidal.
Oh, shit, and what a
wake it will leave.
The lizard's just as
pitiless as it is. I am
pit to the battle of
these grandiose bas-
tards, and I've got
to wall in their
fight. Others have no
place in it. None.
Ha. I get a real kick out of this host.
PARDON ME, MA'AM.
NICE EVENING. BRISK. YES?
HUH?
CKING...
...CRAZY BASTARD!
SHIT!

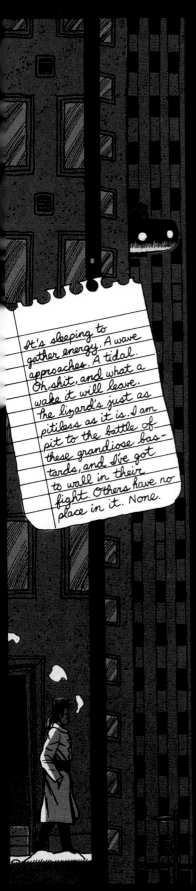

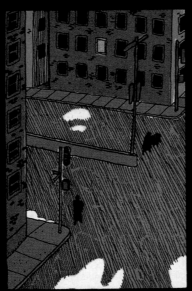

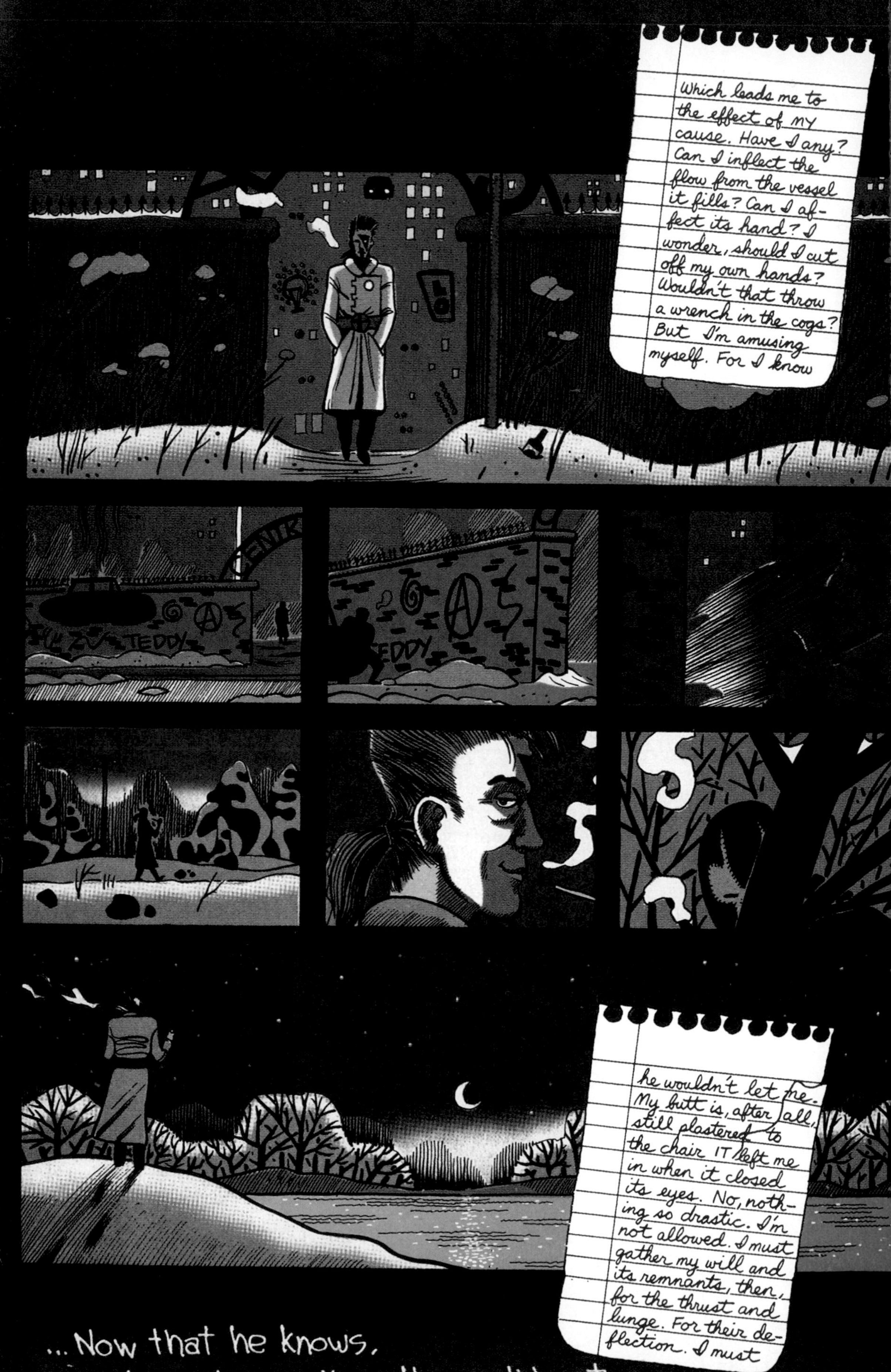
Which leads me to the effect of MY cause. Have I any? Can I inflect the flow from the vessel it fills? Can I affect its hand? I wonder, should I cut off my own hands? Wouldn't that throw a wrench in the cogs? But I'm amusing myself. For I know
TEDDY
TEDDY
he wouldn't let me. My butt is, after all, still plastered to the chair IT left me in when it closed its eyes. No, nothing so drastic. I'm not allowed. I must gather my will and its remnants, then, for the thrust and lunge. For their deflection. I must
...Now that he knows,
he struggles as the others did not.

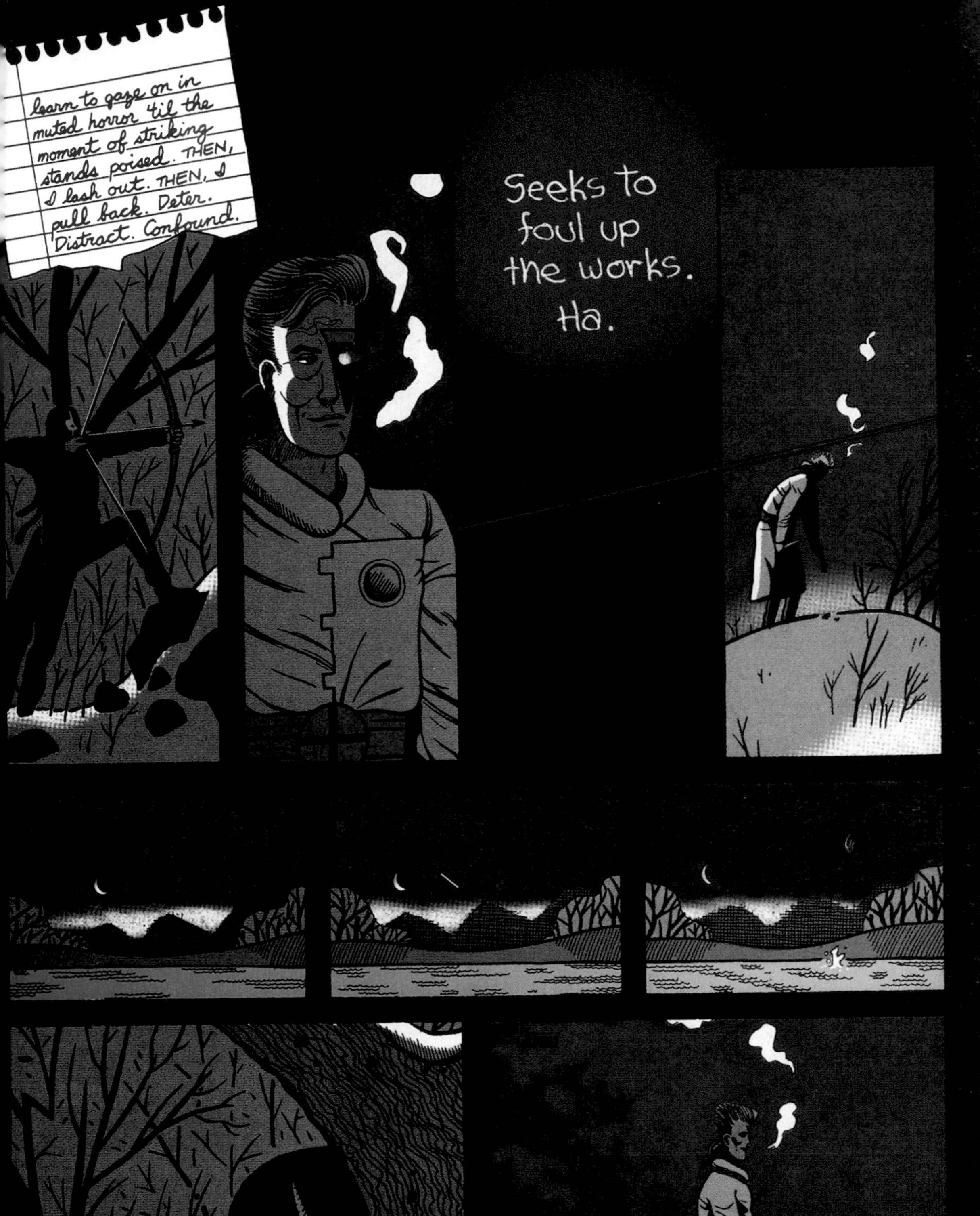
learn to gaze on in muted horror 'til the moment of striking stands poised. THEN, I lash out. THEN, I pull back. Deter. Distract. Confound.
Seeks to foul up the works. Ha.

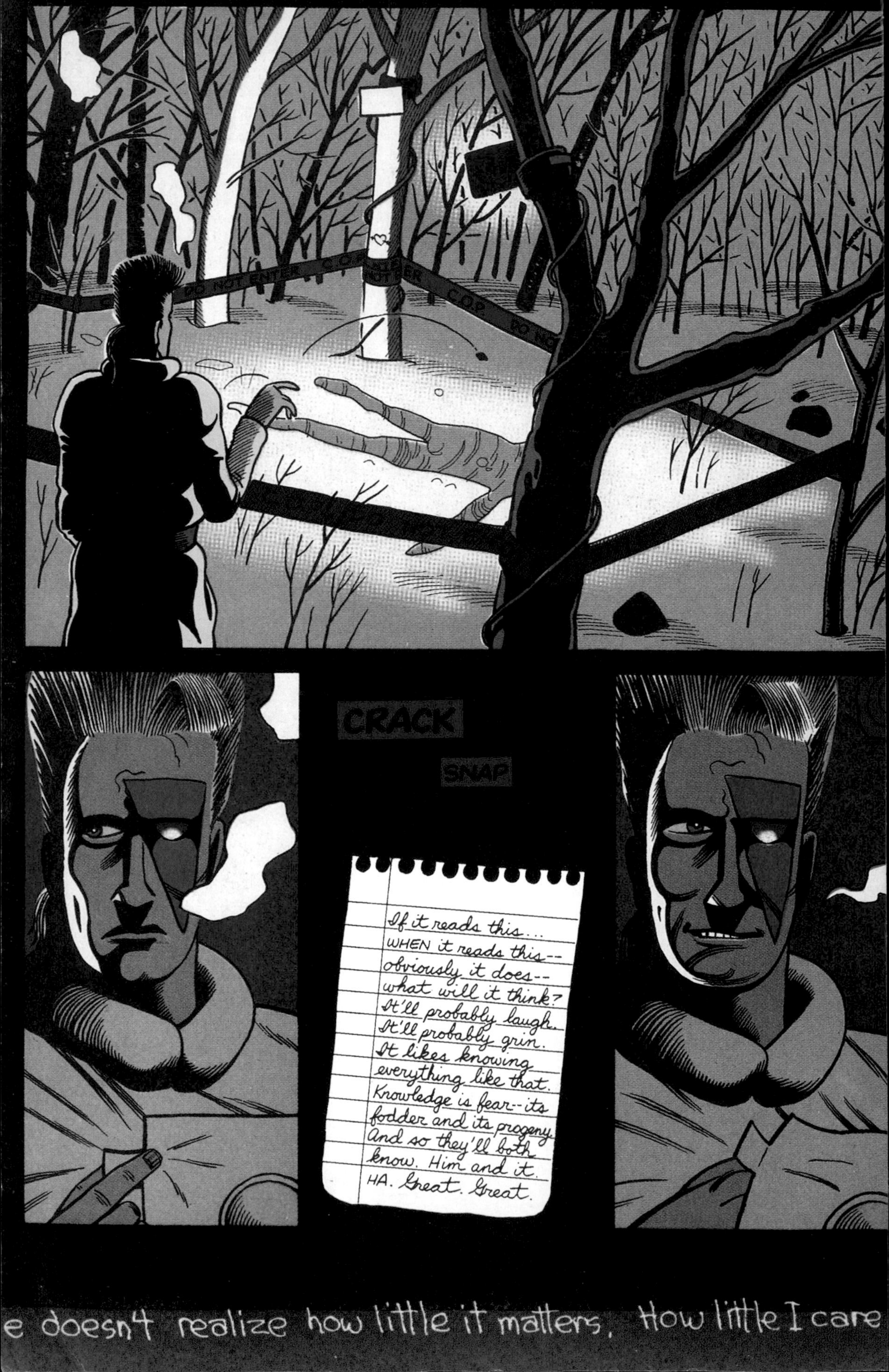
DO NOT ENTER
C.O.P.
CRACK
SNAP
If it reads this...
WHEN it reads this--
obviously it does--
what will it think?
It'll probably laugh.
It'll probably grin.
It likes knowing
everything like that.
Knowledge is fear--its
fodder and its progeny.
And so they'll both
know. Him and it.
HA. Great. Great.

e doesn't realize how little it matters. How little I care

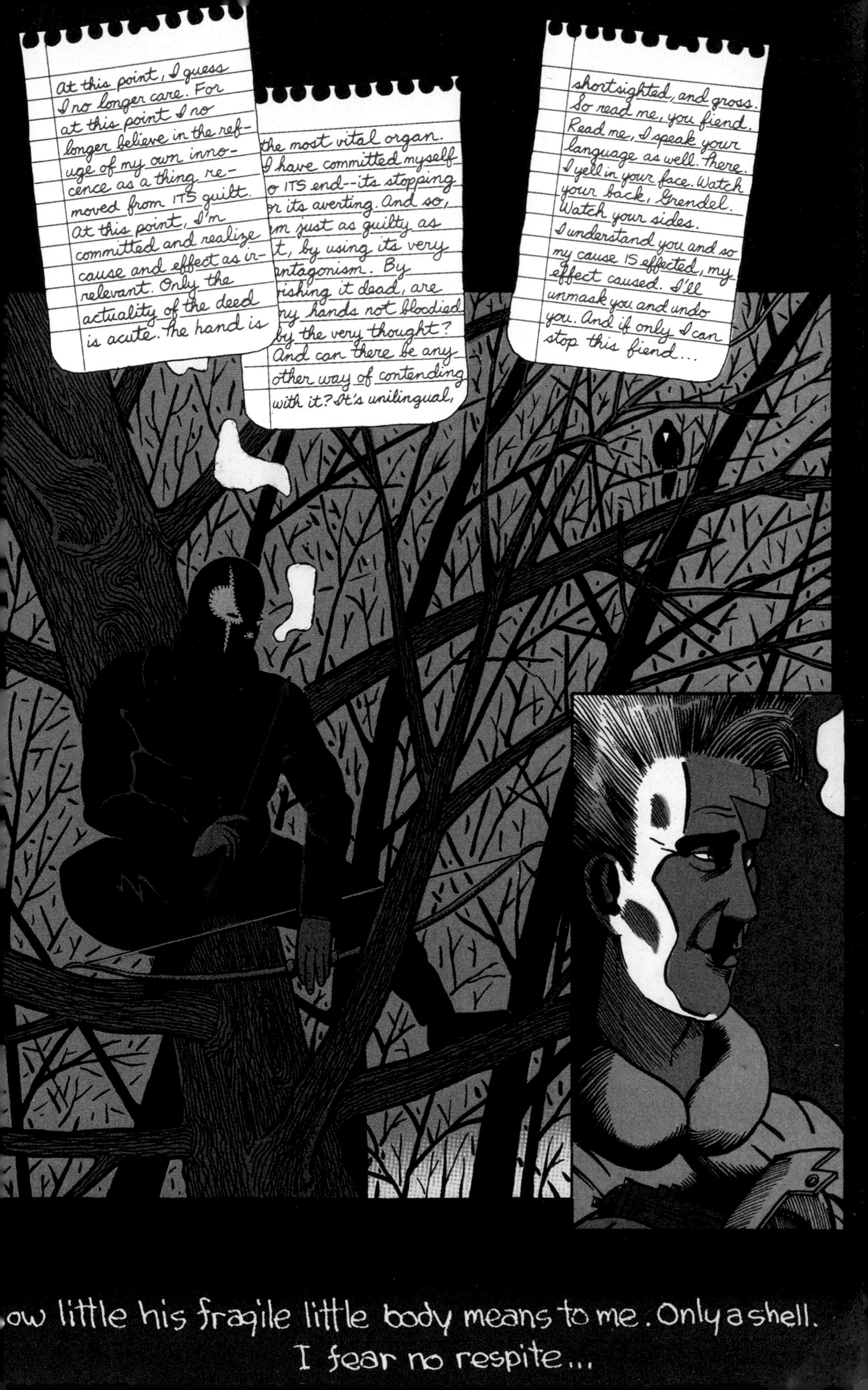
At this point, I guess I no longer care. For at this point I no longer believe in the refuge of my own innocence as a thing removed from ITS guilt. At this point, I'm committed and realize cause and effect as irrelevant. Only the actuality of the deed is acute. The hand is
the most vital organ. I have committed myself
o ITS end--its stopping
r its averting. And so,
m just as guilty as
t, by using its very
antagonism. By
ishing it dead, are
y hands not bloodied
by the very thought? And can there be any other way of contending with it? It's unilingual,
shortsighted, and gross. So read me, you fiend. Read me, I speak your language as well. There. I yell in your face. Watch your back, Grendel. Watch your sides. I understand you and so my cause IS effected, my effect caused. I'll unmask you and undo you. And if only I can stop this fiend...
ow little his fragile little body means to me. Only a shell.
I fear no respite...

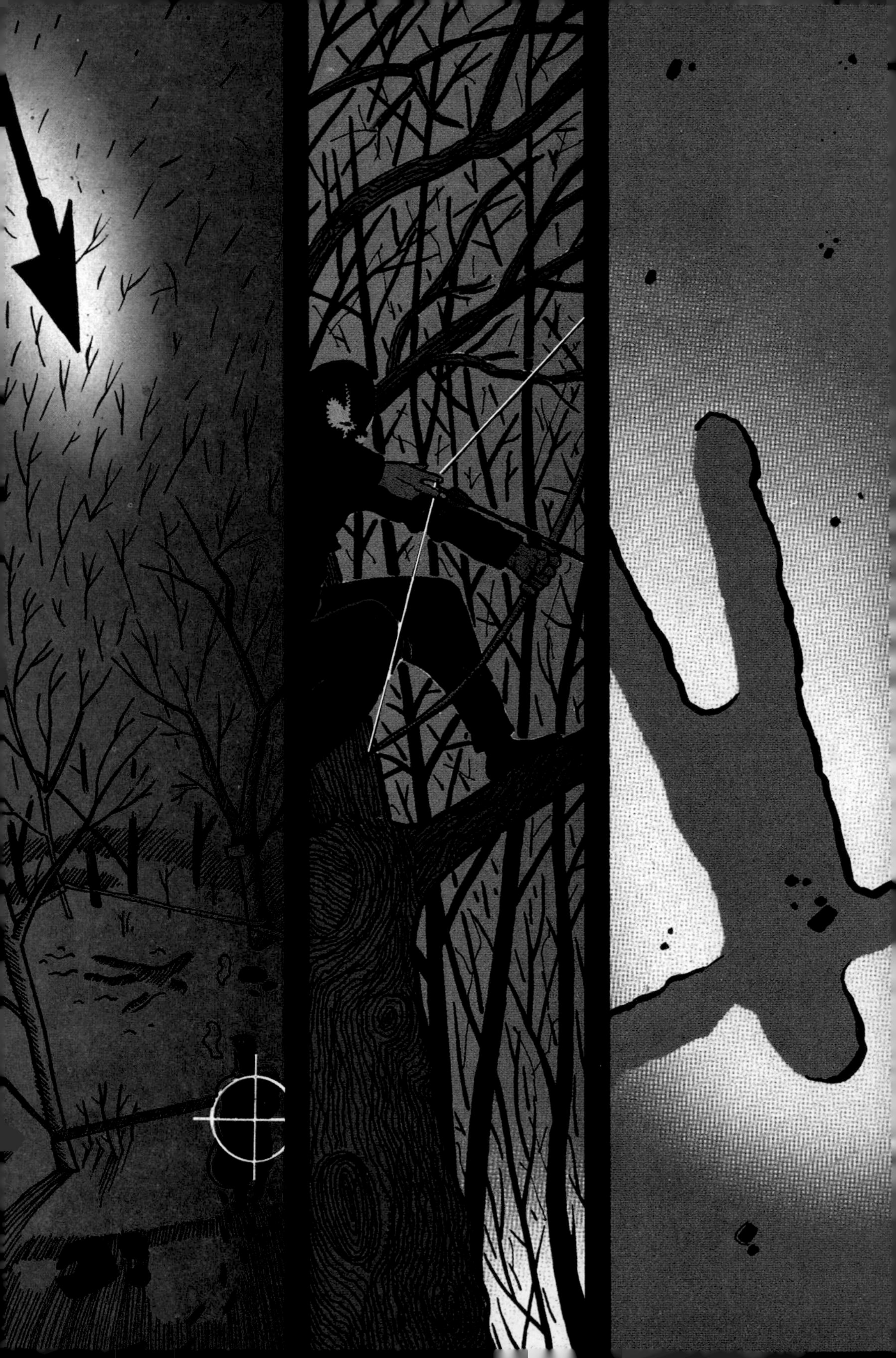

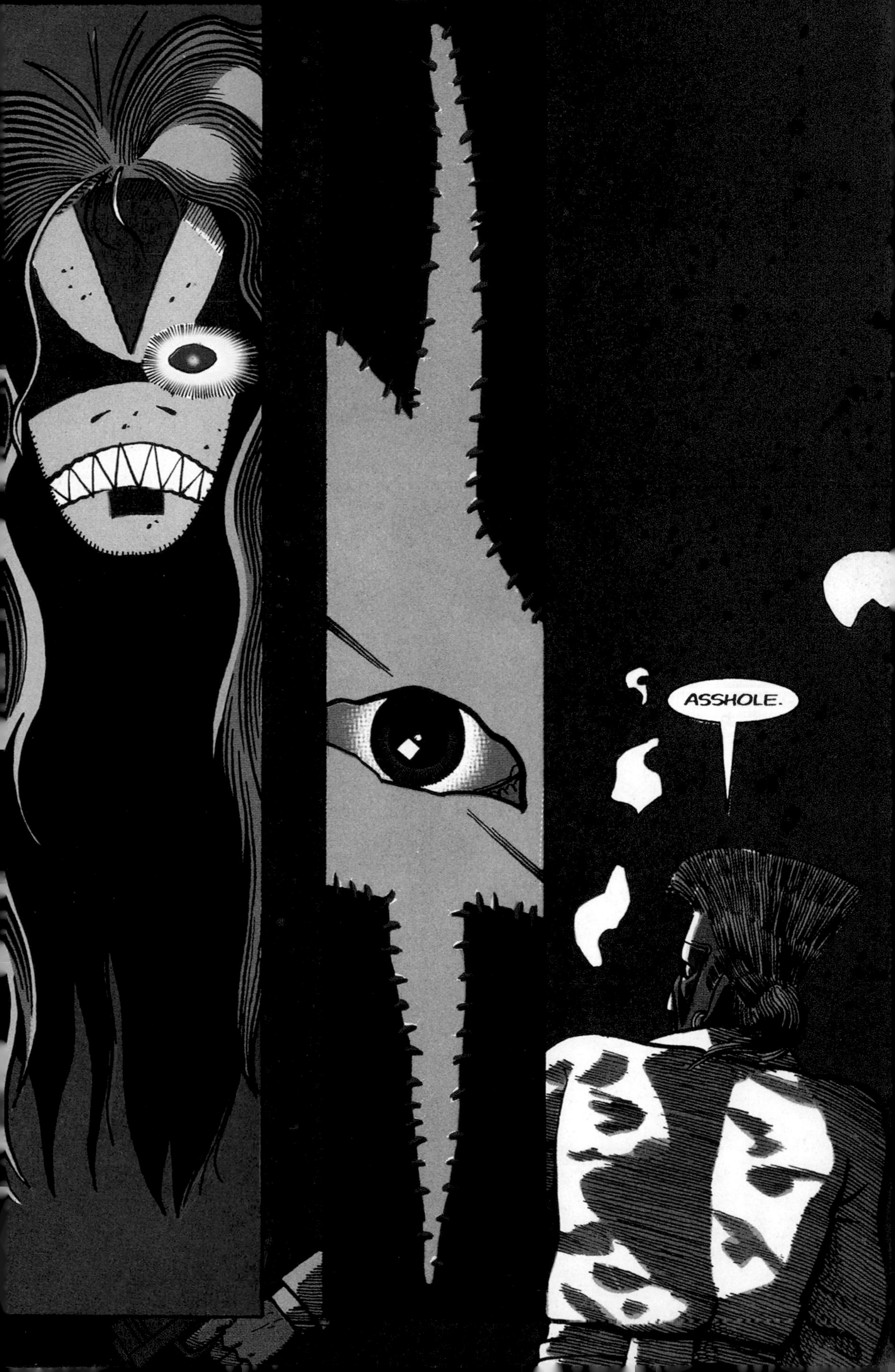
ASSHOLE.

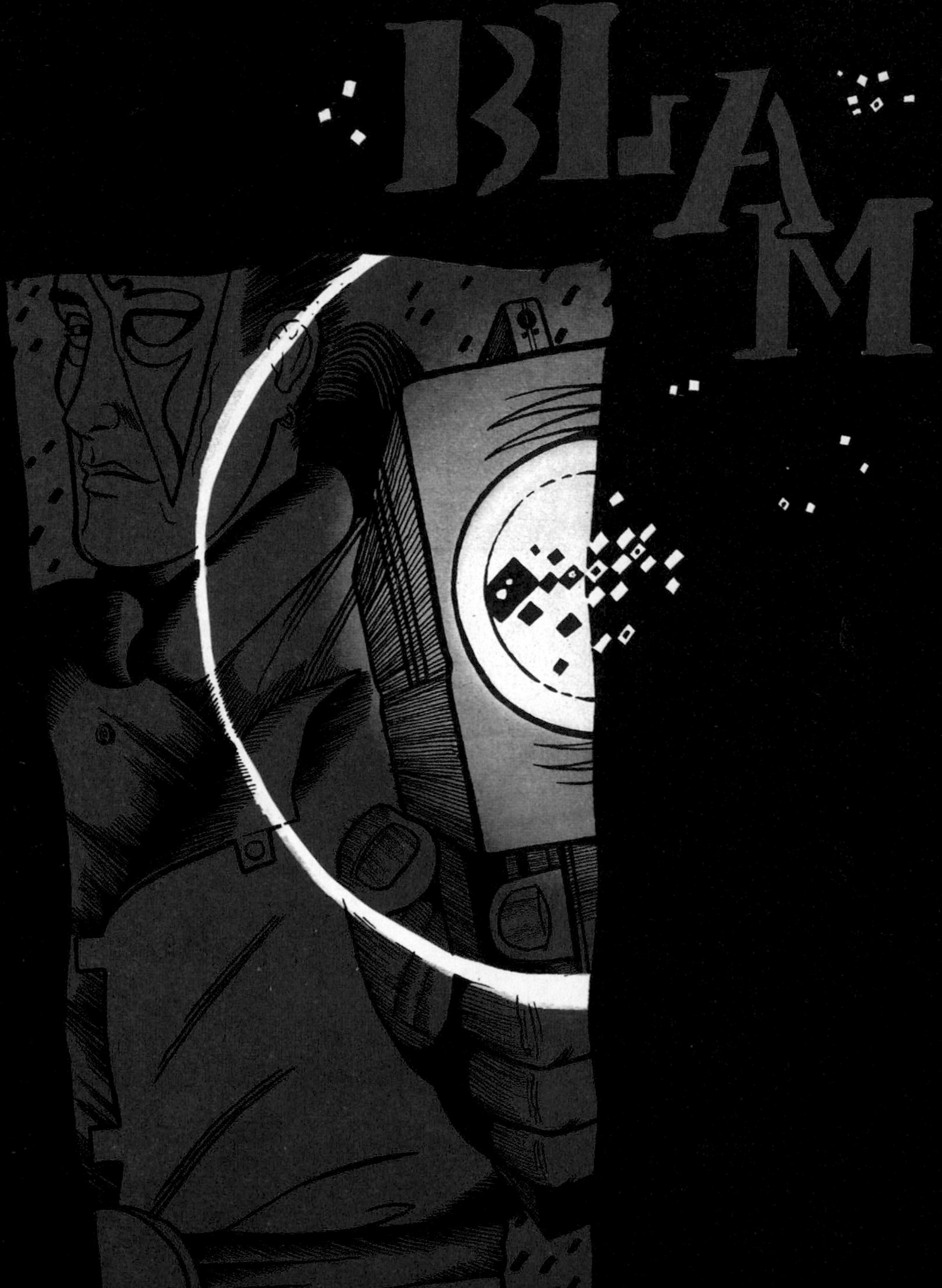
BLAM

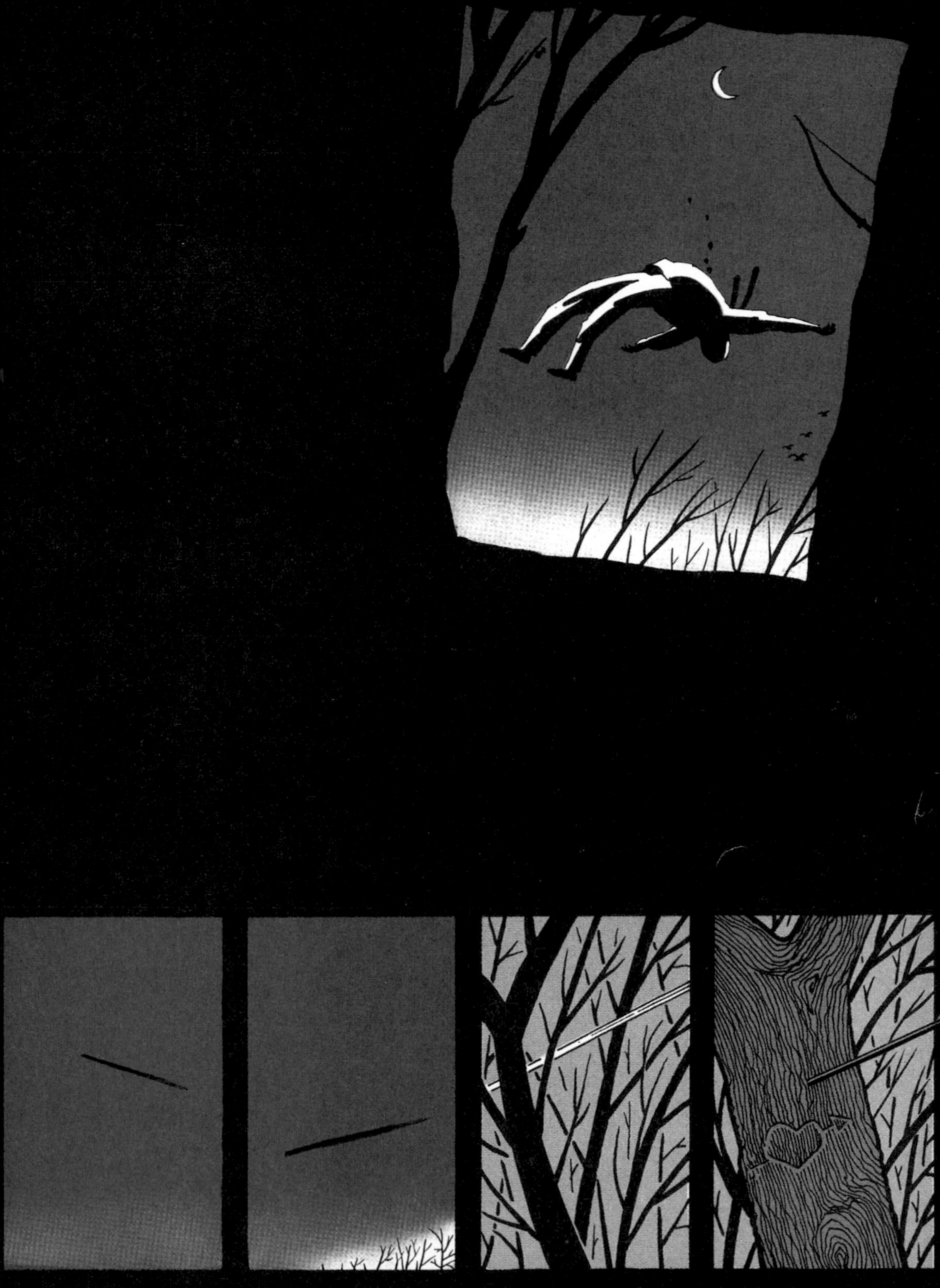

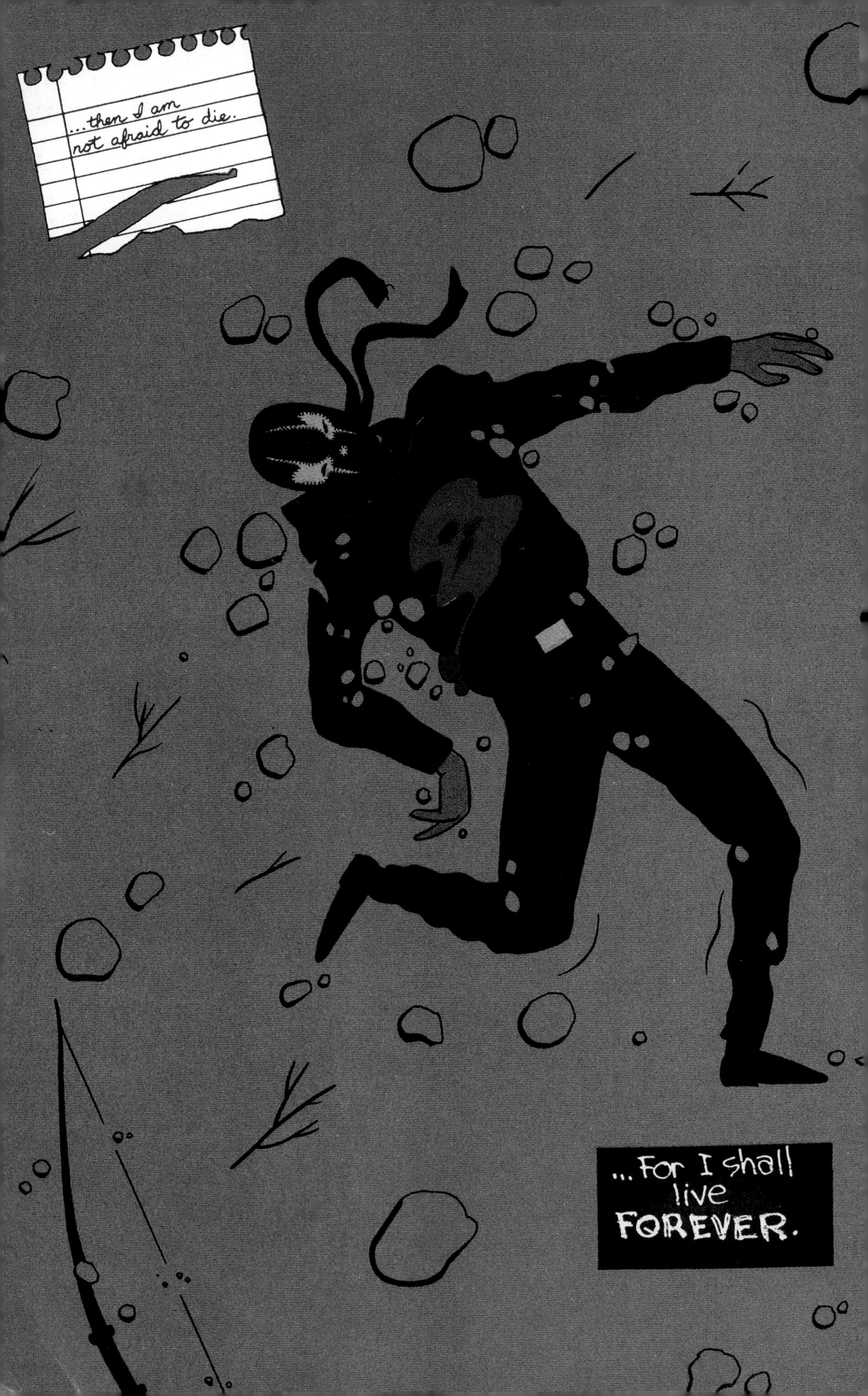
...then I am not afraid to die.
...For I shall live FOREVER.

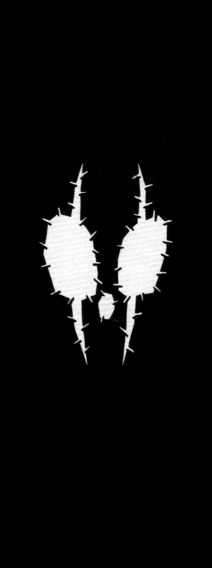

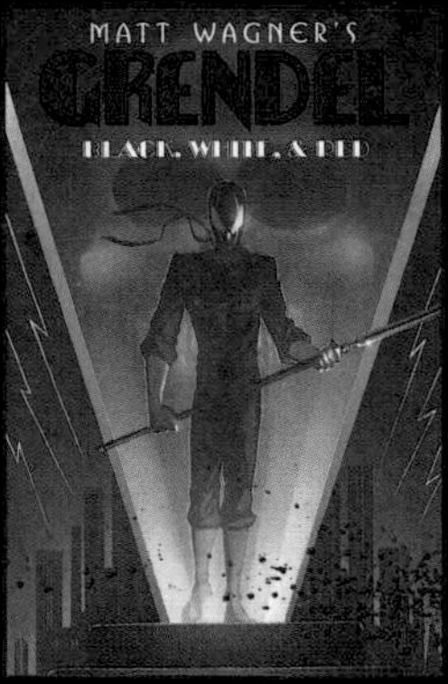
MATT WAGNER'S
GRENDEL
BLACK, WHITE, & RED

Matt Wagner • various artists
200-page two-color paperback
ISBN: 1-56971-493-2 $18.95

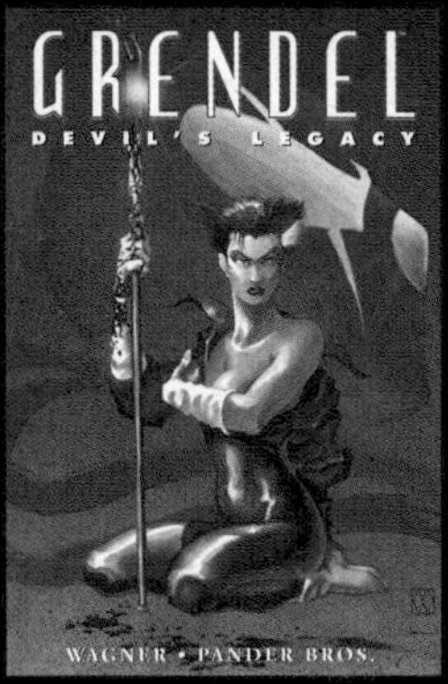
GRENDEL
DEVIL'S LEGACY
WAGNER • PANDER BROS.

Matt Wagner • Pander Bros.
328-page color paperback
ISBN: 1-56971-261-1 $29.95

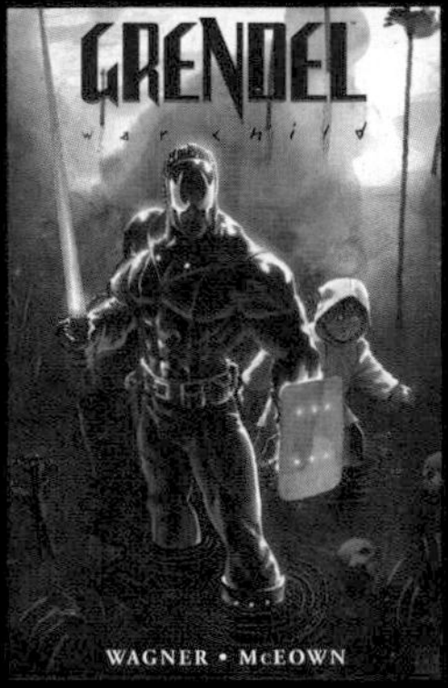
GRENDEL
WAGNER • McEOWN

Matt Wagner • Pat McEown
304-page color paperback
ISBN: 1-878574-89-2 $24.95

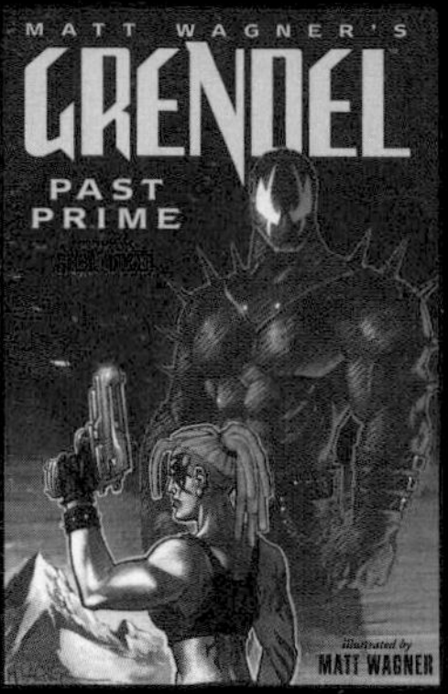
MATT WAGNER'S
GRENDEL
PAST
PRIME
MATT WAGNER

Greg Rucka • Matt Wagner
208-page illustrated novel
ISBN: 1-56971-398-7 $14.95

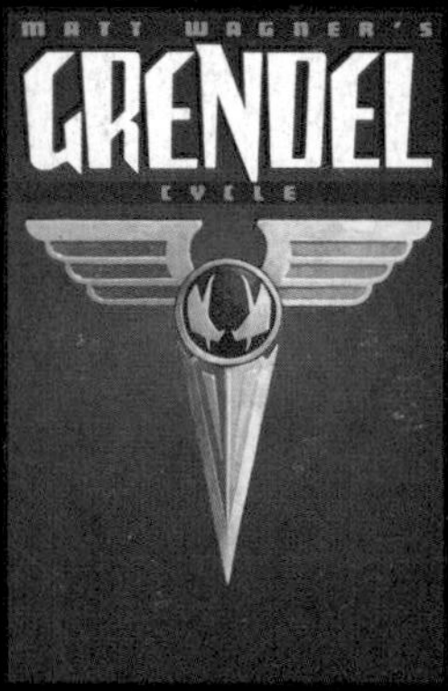
MATT WAGNER'S
GRENDEL
CYCLE

Matt Wagner • various artists
64-page color paperback
ISBN: 1-56971-138-0 $5.95

To find a comics shop in your area, call 1-888-266-4226

FOR MORE INFORMATION OR TO ORDER DIRECT:
•ON THE WEB: www.darkhorse.com
E-MAIL: mailorder@darkhorse.com
•PHONE: 1-800-862-0052 or (503) 652-9701
Mon.-Sat. 9 A.M. to 5 P.M. Pacific Time

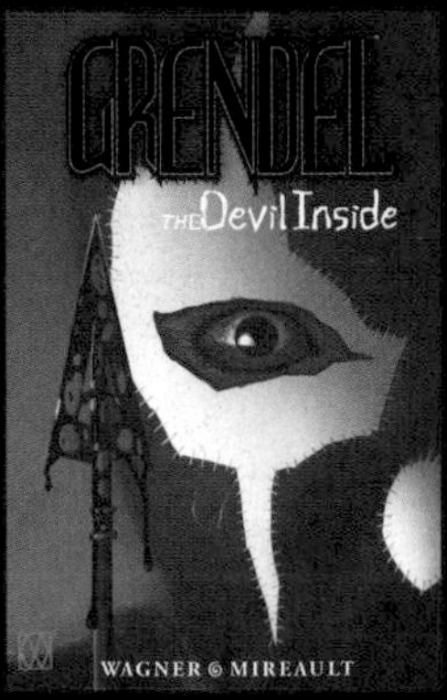
GRENDEL
THE Devil Inside
WAGNER © MIREAULT

Matt Wagner • Bernie Mireault
88-page color paperback
ISBN: 1-56971-604-8 $12.95

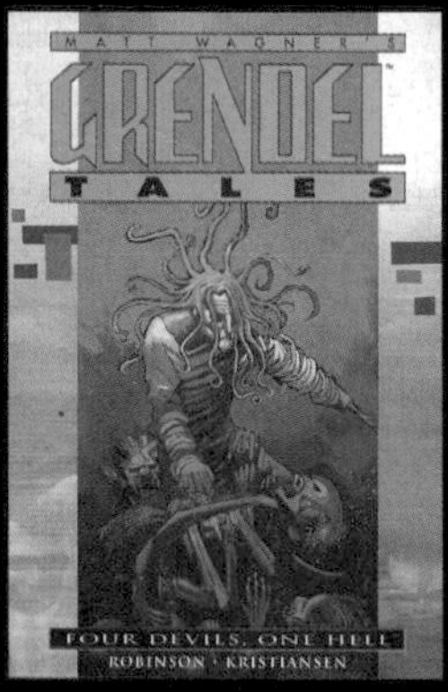
MATT WAGNER'S
GRENDEL
TALES
FOUR DEVILS, ONE HELL
ROBINSON · KRISTIANSEN

James Robinson • Teddy Kristiansen
168-page color paperback
ISBN: 1-56971-027-9 $17.95

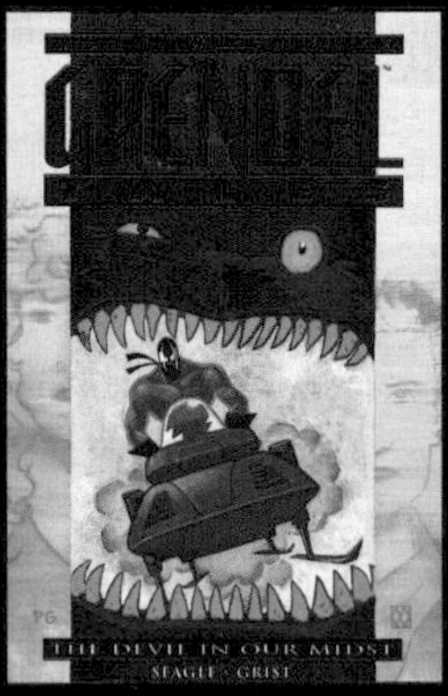
GRENDEL
THE DEVIL IN OUR MIDST
SEAGLE · GRIST

Steven T. Seagle • Paul Grist
136-page color paperback
1-56971-312-X $15.95

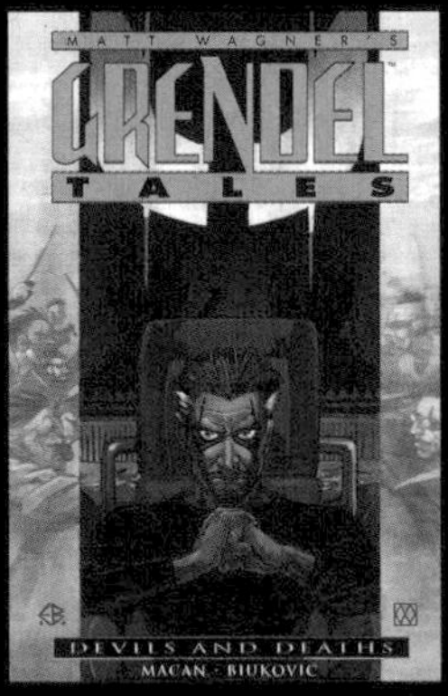
MATT WAGNER'S
GRENDEL
TALES
DEVILS AND DEATHS
MACAN · BIUKOVIC

Darko Macan • Edvin Biuković
160-page color paperback
ISBN: 1-56971-203-4 $16.95

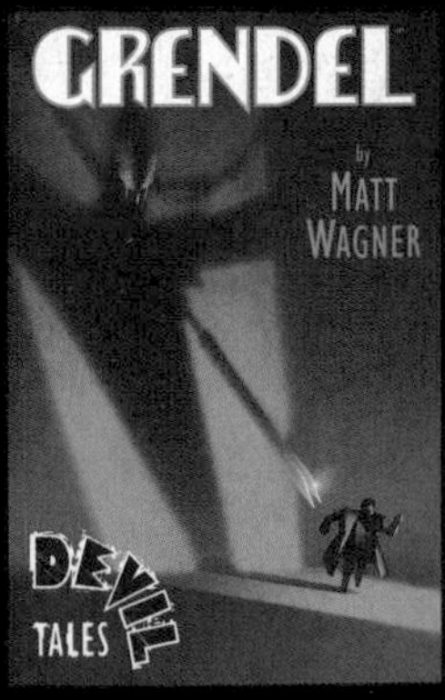
GRENDEL
by
MATT
WAGNER
DEVIL
TALES

Matt Wagner
96-page color paperback
ISBN: 1-56971-428-2 $9.95